Journey to Your Sacred Centre

Listen to the Way, which is called Eternal.

Seeking within, you will find Stillness.

Here, there is no fear or attachment, only Joy and Peace.

Follow the Way and let the dead bury the dead.

It is easier for a camel to pass through the eye of a needle

than for someone attached to this life and

wealth to enter and walk the Way.

ACKNOWLEDGEMENTS

I want to express my deepest gratitude to the Eternal Light of Love for gently guiding me into the soft, still whispers of its Way and allowing me to see the sacred text with eyes of love and for lifting my soul to places that words cannot express.

To my dear wife Laarni, thank you for walking with me every step of the Way with love and patience. To my three beautiful children, Sara, Nathaniel and Daniel, who are like treasures and gifts of loving kindness who confirm what I always felt deep inside. To all my teachers, who taught me the Way. To Mother Earth for her unconditional love and service always. To all my brothers and sisters around the world who walk the *Way of Love* despite all the challenges you face. And to every soul who has sought the heart of God, genuine seekers on the path of Love and Peace, it is to you and for you that I dedicate this book.

My heart intends that every page will fill you with its gentle, loving currents, reminding you of your eternal journey home from the Source and back to the Source (the great **I AM**, **The All**, **Sacred One**, **Cosmic Consciousness**, our **Source**, **God**), the One who breathes through you, the One who is closer than your very breath; the One who formed you with a unique brilliance.

It is for you, my dear friend, that the stars shine, the sun rises and sets, the flowers blossom, and the birds sing. It is to you that I dedicate every sentence of this book. I hope that your spirit-soul will be quickened and moved to search out the beauty and hear the sacred call to find the Sacred Presence, beyond the person, beyond the thoughts, beyond form and religion, and into the infinite, the boundless beauty of the Sacred Light.

CONTENTS

INTRODUCTION

You are about to embark on a journey to seek out the One who breathes life into you, the One who gave you breath and continues to sustain you, and the One to whom you will eventually return. This journey is an eternal process, but I am here to share with you treasures that will help all genuine seekers find true meaning and purpose, and to rediscover the true essence of the All.

I will be quoting from texts of all ages and times, from different cultures, traditions, and teachers, in order to seek and understand the very heartbeat of what the texts are all about, not through the lens of 'self' but through Truth, Spirit, and Light.

Unfortunately, much damage has been done through indoctrination over the centuries and millennia. However, I hope this book sheds some light on the truths of the sacred teachings given by those who have walked the *narrow path*, sacrificing all to find the real treasure worth pursuing until their last breath.

This book is not intended to be a commentary or a textbook, but rather a validation of experiences, quotes, sayings, and sacred texts, through my personal journey of seeking out Truth. Only now, in my fifties, have I finally discovered the hidden treasure buried deep inside. We all have access to this treasure, but most people remain in ignorance and continue to live in spiritual poverty.

My hope in writing this book is to save you time, heartache, and pain, my dear friend. All I ask is for you to have an open mind and heart, to examine, research, and seek out the things I will share. I am not here to tell you what is right or wrong, so you can adopt what I say as Truth. No, no, no! This book is designed to be read and then examined for yourself, not because someone told you or you read about it in a book, but because you have had a personal living experience of it yourself. And as a friend and brother, I am here to help you seek out that hidden treasure laid deep at the core of your being, now and until your last breath.

From your spirit brother,

SB

ABOUT THE AUTHOR

Many people know me for my Satria Fighting Arts (Silat), but that's only one aspect of my life and a small part of who I am. Therefore, let me tell you more about my life so you can understand my journey and what led me to write this book, as my life and this book are intrinsically intertwined. Please bear with me as I unravel some parts of my life. I hope you will find it interesting, and many genuine seekers will be able to relate. So, let's begin...

My journey started in London in 1969, born to a Spanish couple who migrated to London from a little port town called La Linea in Andalucia during the Franco regime. I was raised near the roughest estates of North West London, where racism, crime, and gangs of all races were prevalent. It was a time when the area was designated as a 'project' by the local council, and the estate blocks in the area were home to some of the worst kinds of criminals back in the day. Our house was just around the corner, so I grew up amidst it all. Knowing how to defend myself became a priority, and that's how my journey into martial arts began.

My first encounter with street violence was at the age of five when my Abuela (grandmother) was punched in the face over my school lunchbox as she was walking me to school. Being Spanish meant that we were subjected to racial abuse, and from that point on, getting back and forth from school was a daunting task. The first and worst encounter I recall was when I was eight years old. A group of skinheads beat me up so badly that I was kicked and punched in the face and then forced to eat dog shit, just because I had accidentally kicked my football over a wall where they were standing. This is where my quest to learn self-defence began. I was hungry to know how to fight and defend myself, so I searched for a teacher. At the age of eleven, I was introduced to my first proper martial arts teacher who taught me Kuntao. I trained so much and so hard that I quickly became a good fighter. Although I got bullied less after that, there were always bigger and stronger guys with big egos who wanted to challenge and test my skills, instigating fights. Sadly, the fighting continued.

The first time I experienced sexual abuse was also around five years old when an old Irish man who sat next to me on a bus while my mother sat on a different seat. He put his hands down my shorts, and I remember freezing in my seat. I was scared and confused and was in absolute shock, not understanding what was happening to me by a complete stranger. At another time, I was trying on a jacket in a small local shop's changing area when the shopkeeper locked the main door, pushing and pinning me down to the ground, trying to take my pants down to rape me. Eventually, I freed myself as I bit his finger so hard that he had to let me go.

That experience haunted me for many years in my dreams. I often woke up biting my own finger so hard that it would bleed. Another time, I was on a bus when a group of men surrounded me as I was asleep, speaking abusive words while one tried to push his boot into my private area. There were other incidents I don't need to mention, but I'm sure you get the message. These experiences caused me to shut down so much that I felt dirty for most of my life. Even in my marriage and then becoming a father to our beautiful children, I could still feel the remnants of this horrible sensation and feeling "unclean" for many years after. I often wouldn't come home until I went into a cold-water plunge to feel somehow a bit "cleaner," as I didn't want to pass anything on to my kids.

On top of that, I grew up in a Spanish home where arguing, screaming, shouting, and throwing plates were a regular occurrence. My father was quite abusive with his words, which, after a family incident, became physically abusive as he let out his anger and disappointment on me.

I don't hold any bitterness or anger towards my father, and I never did. In fact, I did his funeral and tried to find only good things to say about him. I had accepted that he was suffering deeply as he lost his own father at a very young age. But growing up in this environment, I found it hard to be at home, so I would often stay out as much as I could. I spent time in the park until it closed, or I would use all my time after school and on weekends playing football. I got so highly skilled at it that I even played professionally for top-level clubs in the UK and Spain while continuing my martial arts training with my Kuntao teacher, whom I trained with from the age of eleven to nineteen years old.

That was the story of my life, and all these experiences led me to an unquenchable thirst to find a way out of it all. But this was all before I met Guru Ma, and only through her did I find a softer way in martial arts. My encounter with her was supernatural. After I had won the National Championship in 1989, I knew my journey with my Kuntao teacher had come to an end. I didn't want this life anymore, so he advised me to do a 7-day rice fast to find a new teacher. I did, and on the 7th day, Guru Ma appeared to me in a vision by a lake at Golders Green. I followed this vision, which eventually and supernaturally led me to her in Holland. She had also told her students about my coming, even before I arrived.

It was the teachings of Guru Ma that had the most significant impact on my life. Through her relationship with God, I saw and experienced things that could not be explained naturally. Her love and closeness to Yeshua was deeply sacred, the most touching and real that I was privileged to witness. I am deeply honoured to have been taken into this part of her life for twenty-three years. At the time, I was still young and could not fully come into her level of consciousness, but she was very patient with me. Unfortunately, she passed away on June 13, 2012, which she had pre-warned me of many years prior, saying that she would hold out until 2012, and that, she certainly did!

Guru Ma knew many things about my life; she could see right through my soul. As a young man, her presence scared me, but I knew she was carrying something that I needed in my life and that I had been searching for all my life. She took me in like a son, although I completely respected her as my teacher until we became close like friends in her later years. She taught me many things, all esoteric-based. But at the time, most of it went over my head as I only wanted to train the Silat.

Over the years of studying under her teachings, she would teach on biblical prophecies, too, warning me about events on the globe that would take place during my time. You see, at her school, I couldn't just attend the Silat classes, I had to participate in her esoteric lectures and text studies, where she would go through middle-eastern texts such as the Bible and the Qu-ran, Buddhist texts written in Sanskrit and Pali, an ancient Indian collection of Vedic Sanskrit texts like the Rigveda and the Bhagavad Gita, and then there was the book of nature as well as people's lives. She had a way of going over fine details in scriptures or texts and finding the thread that connected them all. She didn't miss a single point and did this with everything in her life.

During this period, I also met my beautiful wife, Laarni, and we have three children. During this time, I also encountered messengers here on earth and messengers from another dimension. I could write about them all here, but I want to follow the purpose of this book. Despite all the amazing, out-of-this-world testimonies around me, there were still things in my heart and mind that didn't feel whole, and a deep longing remained. So I practised meditation and prayer for hours and hours, explored Buddhism, and studied a lot of Buddhist texts. I was on a more profound quest to find out the Truth of my existence and all existence, which led me to a search to find God. And this was what my soul had longed for since I took my first breath. Growing up, I always had a deep sense of another way of life, an inner life, but I lost my way. I tried many things, even drugs, but nothing filled that gap. The scars that had marred me from all the abuse I experienced were deeply embedded in me, and not even my teacher, Guru Ma, could deliver me. Then, just before my 50th birthday and just before COVID-2019 occurred, events started to happen in my life, and I began to experience awakenings.

Then, in 2020, something hit me like a ton of bricks. I finally woke up! Reality and its true nature had hit me, and it was a EUREKA moment. I found myself hitting my head, wondering why I had not seen this before. I realized that I was already what I had been searching for all my life! The presence that I could feel in others or moments of no mind and letting go was within me. I was in the light, in this awareness, and it was me all along! This light exists beyond reason, thoughts, and ego, with all its constructs, ideas, beliefs, and struggles. I had completely rejected the idea that I could be clean and whole, which prevented me from settling into this beautiful presence. I could not abide in this state, nor could I rest there. I believed it was possible for others, but not for myself. Finally, when I gave up, when I came to the end of myself and stopped trying, it happened. I suddenly found myself enveloped in the most beautiful, formless, and invisible presence, without effort, strain, or trying. I knew fully, wholeheartedly, that this was my true "Self" that I had searched for all my life. At that moment, the following text became real for me:

> You are the light of the world. A city that is set on a hill cannot be hidden.
>
> Nor do they light a lamp and put it under a basket, but on a lampstand,
>
> and it gives light to all *who are* in the house.
>
> -   Gospel of Matthew 5:14

I was truly experiencing my **true essence**, an essence that was fully satisfied and content just being here. It didn't need anything more added to it. It was perfectly whole as it always had been! Yet, there I was, trying to find it, attempting to experience it through the vehicle of the mind, with more and more effort. And yet, it was always there, patiently waiting for me to come home, calling me back with loving-kindness like a caring friend or a lover. Finally, after years of striving and pushing, I was home. My search was over. I understood the meaning of being "lost" and "found." It didn't require any effort, confession of faith, esoteric tantric exercises, mysterious plants, drugs, long fasts, hours of praying, or meditating. I was simply **letting go** of all attempts to be anything other than myself in the present moment.

An incredible sensation of bliss enveloped my entire body as I bathed in this blissful Presence with the most unconditional waves of loving kindness. All the dirty and unclean feelings I had felt in my body that had plagued me for years had melted like wax. And this was only the beginning, but the right beginning, because any other foundation or beginning other than WE ARE IT, requiring nothing other than to **let go** of all trying, will only spin you in the wrong direction. We are IT. We are that which illuminates. We are the substance, our essence without form, empty of 'self' yet full of radiant Presence. We are the Light of Awareness that is a lamp unto our feet, the all-knowing Presence, the Light of Awareness that knows absolute reality and transcends the limiting concepts and ideas of the ego self. And all we have to do is **STOP**. Stop trying to be anything. The moment we give up and let go, is the moment Life will surface and reveal itself. I had read **Luke 17:33** and finally understood its meaning. Yeshua spoke:

> Whoever tries to save his life will lose it, and whoever loses his life will preserve it.

When we wholeheartedly give up trying to cling to life and fully accept **"I am this"** without any judgment, Presence, by the very nature of Presence, reveals itself. And when it does, that is your new life's end and the beginning. As you move further into the pages of this book, it will become apparent that **no effort** is required to journey through life without having to fear it or feel that you are trapped, or, like me, who thought I was an utter failure covered in the stench of filth. Honestly, I was the soul covered in sinking sand, trying with every fibre of me, struggling to fight my way out but only sinking deeper and deeper into the muck until I got tired of trying and eventually just gave up. And you, too, can give up. But don't just take my word for it. Instead, closely examine the words and test them for yourself. Why? Because there are and have always been deceptive teachers with wrong motives leading people astray. In all walks of life and not just in religious circles. We have all encountered misinformation, lies, gossip, and coverups. So, it's our responsibility to seek, knock, and ask the right questions until we have tested everything and are thoroughly convinced. I am not asking you to adopt my views or change your belief system. Instead, I invite you to remain open but test and examine everything with humility and sincerity.

May every page bring you closer to your True Self, the most authentic you, until you re-discover the beautiful union you can access, which is your sovereign right.

Live in tune with the Universal Soul,

Let this be the final craving you cherish.

Let this be your last prayer.

Cast off your separate ego and merge

in the Universal Entity.

Let there be no distance, no distinction;

Every particle of the human body is a symbol

of Universal Existence.

Creation is the image of the Creator,

The experience of unity is the fulfilment of human endeavours.

- Rigveda 8.44.2

THE TWELVE PETALS OF OUR HEARTS

In the ancient text, our hearts are called many things: carriers of Sacred Truth, a secret resting place for the Light of Love to dwell in; or as the Prophet Jeremiah wrote, *"I will put my Law within them, and I will write it on their hearts"* confirming that we are carriers of **Divine Truth**. Yeshua said, *"Blessed are those who have a pure heart for they shall see God"*, describing a pure heart as the gateway to the mysterious Presence of God. Rumi, the great poet, said, *"I looked in temples, churches and mosques, but found the Divine within my heart"*, again confirming our hearts are the resting place for the **Divine Spark**.

In the ancient language of Sanskrit, our hearts are called 'Anahata', which means *unhurt, unstruck*, or *unbeaten*, associating our hearts with the potential for balance, harmony, and peace. However, many people worldwide, of all ages, tribes, and tongues, often complain of a broken, heavy, and weary heart. Is it possible that our precious and sacred hearts are purposed for something entirely different from what we have been taught or conditioned to believe? Is there another way for our hearts to journey on this beautiful planet, and are we not paying attention to its gentle whispers? Could it be that we have tied our hearts to the wrong things, and now, they have become *worried and anxious*, rather than *light and easy*, as the ancient text describes them, with the potential to love wholeheartedly and find rest and refuge in times of trouble? Could it be that there is another pace and rhythm that our beautiful, loving, pure hearts want to travel in, yet we are pushing them like a cart horse instead of treating them like a gentle, loving friend?

Let's explore this together and journey through every page to discover the potential of what lies **within us** and **who we are**. But before we do, let's ponder for a moment on what inspires the flower to open and blossom, the sunflower to follow the sun, the birds with their remarkable ability to design and make such intricate nests, or the inspiration behind the beautiful colours we see when the sun sets or rises. As you ponder this, ask yourself what things may open your tender heart to create beautiful colours, write a new song, create a new life, or express a loving gesture or a kind word. We all feel that our hearts are the central place of immense potential, a place where rich qualities and abilities may lie dormant, misdirected, or even closed and afraid to open. Pain can do many things to humans, and not managing our pain and suffering will most definitely because the heart to do many things other than open and follow its true, authentic sound.

So, what is this original sound, the **Divine** that Rumi was referring to? All these great souls spoke of the **Buddha Nature**, the **Christ within**, or the **Divine Self** when describing our true hearts. One of the most comforting ways of being with your heart and learning to discover its true qualities is to treat it with the most gentle, unconditional, loving kindness, as though it were your very best friend! Treating your heart as your best friend may be something you have never heard of or considered. But if the ancient mystics were right and our hearts were the resting place for the Divine, a place of rest and refuge, then we should start paying more attention to it.

Perhaps it's time to create a sacred space for it to reveal itself—a place and environment where your precious heart can once again breathe in as though it were resting on a carpet of Love with a space to explore without pointing the finger at it and without having to be right or wrong. To be in an environment that is open to making mistakes without fear of failure or being shouted at; a place without fear, guilt, shame, and condemnation; a space free from all the harsh judgments you have made about yourself. Instead, open up an area where your innermost secrets feel safe without judgement. A sacred space within where the heart is allowed to be what it is and express what it wants; an area where it can begin to dance again, where you enter in just as you are, a space where there is no need to hide or cover oneself; a space where the masks are removed, and all the defence mechanisms can finally drop. It's clear why the ancients described this place as the **Secret Place**. Because it is a place where one can be naked, broken, vulnerable, or whatever they are in this moment, with an accepting embrace so that the Divine Spark may appear and breathe until you finally arrive home.

We are meant to be **here**, to enjoy the sunsets, beautiful skies, night sky, and the wonderful forests. We were designed for this place, and this place was made for us. Can you imagine sensing your precious heart being given this space with total acceptance? How it would begin to experience its true authentic qualities, described as petals, as though your beautiful heart was brightly coloured outside like a beautiful flower and stemming forth with a fragrance, carrying the essence and ability to create and form such beauty. These *twelve petals* are named and experienced as *Joy, Peace, Love, Compassion, Kindness, Gentleness, Forgiveness, Patience, Unity, Harmony, Purity, and Bliss.*

Let's explore what happens when we experience one of these twelve petals. Let's say we choose Love and apply it to ourselves, including all our past mistakes. Love would automatically birth forgiveness, peace, understanding, and so on. This wheel of petals would spin and move with force, a power that brings healing to troubled hearts. Science has been able to prove that our heart energy can reach others, so the wheels would keep spinning and creating a powerful cycle within all of us. This cycle would touch our circle of friends, families, and communities, bringing restoration. This power is contained in our hearts, but it must happen within us first. It starts by creating a space of acceptance for our hearts to breathe freely again.

CHAPTER 1

OUR CALLING

From The One That Calls

People often mistake a "calling" for their skills, jobs, dreams, or ambitions. But, to know one's calling, you must go beyond these external factors. In fact, in a person's life, one will encounter many jobs and opportunities and may often change careers. A desire for true Love will influence some, while others will be affected for purely economic reasons. Sometimes, jobs change because of age, and so can dreams. So then, what is one's calling?

Your inner calling is not your job, vocation, or dream, as these things are determined by many factors and often influenced by many things. However, they are significant in the stability and anchoring of one's life, especially in this ever-changing and highly competitive material world we all live in. The cost to live here does not match the seed that falls into the ground freely and grows into a beautiful apple or pear tree for free! My simple advice on this would be to quote the words of Rumi:

> When you are immersed in pursuits that you enjoy
> wholeheartedly, illness and pain won't distract you.
>
> - Rumi

What Rumi is saying, in other words, is: choose a job, career or vocation that feels more like an extended vacation. Something that would make you jump out of bed to do. Something that would put a smile on your face so that you can put a smile on others' faces too.

A calling is something more profound. There needs to be a Caller that is calling and a Caller that needs to be discerned. Could we already carry the wonders we seek inside ourselves and are searching in the wrong places?

Humans are constantly searching for more and more, as though there is a force that is never quenched, never quite satisfied, never fully contented like a wildfire fuelled with an increasing desire to have more, to know more, to be more. But what if we were enough? And the way was in and not out? What if the way was through our sacred hearts and not through this everchanging, constantly demanding material world?

The ancients called our hearts the **resting place**—a space within us where we can abide, settle, and find proper, satisfying rest. A place where we could recover from a long and tricky journey. A place where we can find strength in times of trouble. But how can we know unless we venture and take a step in this direction? How would we ever discover that this Light would not take ten steps towards us if we didn't make that step? If we are sincerely honest, most of us have been too busy chasing the material world when the material world is only ever moving further and further away, and we are only ever losing strength in the chasing process.

We are all here with different faces, names, and stories seeking joy, happiness, and peace. The proof that we seek lies deep within us, waiting to be explored and experienced. There is a story in one of the gospels where Yeshua is explaining to Martha that all her hard work and effort are not required and will only be a distraction, and instead, what her sister Mary is doing is the only thing needed.

As Yeshua and his disciples were on their way, he came to a village where a woman named Martha opened her home to him. She had a sister called Mary, who sat at the Lord's feet listening to what he said. But Martha was distracted by all the preparations that had to be made. She came to him and asked, "Lord, don't you care that my sister has left me to do the work by myself? Tell her to help me!". "Martha, Martha," the Lord answered, "you are worried and upset about many things, but few things are needed or indeed only one. Mary has chosen what is better, and it will not be taken away from her."

- Gospel of Luke 10:38-42

Yeshua is pointing out that she (*Martha*) is getting upset and worried over nothing, thus, losing her peace. But, meanwhile, Mary found the eternal sacred moment that is here and now and that has always been; something that cannot be taken away from her because it's the very substance that she is, the very essence that she carries, is her central eternal Presence, the Light of her soul, the life that was breathed into her; something that cannot be earned by good works, points, merit, or from striving. But instead, it is a gift. The gift of **who** we are, **what** we are, the gift of our sacred Light, our uniqueness, the gift of the Sacred Presence. This Sacred Presence can be easily missed or misplaced, lost in our pursuit of fame and glory, or sold over for fleeting pleasures that tickle our emotions and forge destructive habits. This calling is often called and described as the *Great Way*, or the *Great Tao*, the *Path* leading us to *Eternal Life*—our journey that we all need to make and discover, and with the help of all the past great teachers who were pointing to it, we too can return.

Enter through the narrow gate. For wide is the gate, and broad is the road

that leads to destruction, and many enter through it. But small is the gate

and narrow the road that leads to life, and only a few find it.

- Matthew 7:13

The Way is described as a narrow gate and a narrow path, and broad is the way of distraction, quickly causing us to miss this sacred moment of our lives. We must first **get ourselves out** of the way to find the way of the sacred calling. It is not something we can grasp with our hands, but rather, allowing ourselves to be held, enabling the breath to breathe us as it once did. This is "getting out of the way so that the Way can surface". It sounds like a mystery, a paradox, but if you allow life to be without discrimination or judgment, then life, by the nature of life, will most certainly reveal its fragrance to you.

Listen to the Way, which is called Eternal

- Upanishads

We are encouraged to go within and find stillness, beyond the cares of this world, beyond the noise of our fears and anxieties and into the dimension of abiding peace, where we can listen to its whispers and find wisdom.

Those who find the Way are those who have

Love and forgiveness in their hearts.

- Bhagavad Gita

Those with a pure heart, and who seek the Way without ceasing
will find it. It is like cleansing glass until the dust is removed. Seeking
within, you will find stillness. Here there is no more fear or
attachment, only joy.

- Dhammapada

The secret of the Way waits for those who have overcome desire.

- Tao Te Ching

In every tradition, the **Way**, the **Sacred Calling** has been described uniquely, giving the reader clues and inspiration regarding the requirements. By introducing these small, peaceful, and gentle whispers, I aim to remind you that your life is not only about making a living, working, or raising a family because there is much more to life than just that. There is a *sacred calling* that can form a **union**, **oneness** with your beautiful, precious heart where the Love and Light of the one who created you in your mother's womb and called you before the foundation of the earth can surface, allowing your original, naked, and beautiful **true face** to come forth. Your authentic and unique sound can burst through and into your life, freely expressing itself without interference. Total acceptance plays itself out in a world that is desperately trying to shape our experience of life into its own image and likeness so that it can better fit in and serve the material world. This worldly way often obstructs the path of the *Way*. **We are** meant to be who we truly are, as we were created and destined to become, rather than who we have been forced, conditioned, or brainwashed to be. Our **true essence** has always been present, waiting to reveal itself like the sun setting and rising, giving life to all around and mirroring its authentic nature simply by being the sun. So, what is our calling? Our calling is to shine, to illuminate this world with our original, undefiled, and unwavering Presence, like a lamp that naturally lights up a room, allowing others to see and enter. Our calling is for our Light to shine before others, so that all who come into contact with this Light will naturally see their reflection and feel the peace and Love that resides within.

Indeed, this beautiful process begins within our hearts first. It starts by responding to its promptings to come home and find rest. It's a prompting to return to deep stillness where the space within is textured with loving-kindness, and the whispers are like those of a true and faithful friend who has always been there, patiently waiting for their best and most intimate friend to return home.

BEFORE WE WERE BORN

In the ancient Hebrew book of the seer, Jeremiah is told that he was already known even before he took incarnation here on Earth:

The word of the Lord came to me, saying, "before I formed you
in the womb I knew you, before you were born, I set you apart I
appointed you as a prophet to the nations."

- Book of Jeremiah 1:4-5

There is indeed a place beyond our understanding of time and space, a place described as the **heart** and **mind** of the **Creator**. It's a place of eternal existence where our **original face** and Presence were intimately existing as the breathing heartbeat of God, waiting for the right time to take incarnation and experience life through the miracle of our bodies, anatomy, and physiology.

This points to a place beyond culture, tribes, beliefs, ideas, religion, and identity. It's a place where we pre-existed without form, a place of pure bliss and Light where we rest within and through the Source.

For in Him we live and move and have our being.

- Book of Acts 17:28

We are not our bodies, we are not our thoughts, and we are not our place of birth. To know this, we have to enter into what Jeremiah revealed - that our true nature, our true image, and our likeness are in the very heart and mind of Eternity, born from a time and place beyond form, beyond attachment, beyond the grasping mind, and into a dimension of empty universal space where Light and Love travels freely. It sounds too fantastical, but even our bodies comprise 99.99999% of space and energy. This confirms that all is empty sound vibration, with nothing to grasp, yet nothing has arrived by accident.

Jeremiah reveals a beautiful secret: we are not the products of chance or luck but rather of a life with a purpose, a calling, and a destiny. Your life has a story, with meaning and chapters of pure experience unfolding like pages in a book. You, my dear friend, are beautifully original and breathed into with a loving universal cosmic force and have a unique role to play here on this beautiful planet.

The Source reveals to Jeremiah that it is time for him to accept his place here on Earth as though it whispers, "*settle my son, and take your place. You were born for this time. Accept your role, accept yourself as you are, as you came, you are not an accident, different like every grain of sand or fingerprint yet perfect just as you are.*"

Jeremiah reveals our True Face before our parents were even born, like asking a flower what it was before it was a flower. So, when the text describes us as lost, it says we have lost our true image and likeness. Very much like the story Yeshua tells of a woman searching for a lost coin, and upon finding it, she rejoices and is overwhelmed with bliss and happiness *(Luke 15:8–10)*.

Both ancient and modern coins have this one thing in common: they both have images on them—a face. In the Vedas, the path home is beautifully described like this:

I now realise the Presence of the One, the universal entity who is

self-illuminated and radiant like the sun. He is beyond all darkness, now I

fear not even death. I proclaim this is the path, the only path to peace,

to the goal of life, eternal bliss.

~ Vedas (Yaju 31.18)

To understand the way home is to trust and find rest in the hands of a loving Source whose Light is genuinely radiant, universal, beyond all darkness and fear, and waiting to reveal itself to us as we journey home to the centre of our hearts. Before we took shape and form, we pre-existed in the universal loving heart of unconditional Love that is ever-sustaining and shaping the entire map of the Universe. It is here that we can sit in deep stillness, understanding that we are eternal beings. There is no need to fear death or the sting of death. Instead, our lives are part of an extraordinary existence, with a much grander plan than we could imagine, and a far more incredible journey towards the Light and into the Light, for we are spirit and Light. That is who we are, my dear friends: we are all specs of this divine Light journeying back to the centre. So take a deep breath and reflect on this for a moment before you turn to the next page.

You are loved deeply, more profoundly than you have ever experienced, and much further than your wild imagination can expand to. Trust and allow the work that began in you to continue. The majestic work of creation that formed you in the womb of your dear mother continues until now. Let go and allow this life to be eternal, this cosmic Life Force that is super creative and intelligent, to carry you through every chapter, trial, and page of your life. The Light that began a good work in you will be faithful to take you home. Feel the carrying force of a caring, loving hand moving your life from one moment to the next until you feel that it is breathing you, and there is nothing more to do, nothing to prove, nowhere to get to, and nothing to become because, as you are, you are perfect and have always been perfect.

So, rest. Really find rest and sit with the mountains, sit alongside the sun and the moon, and sit with Mother Earth. Be your authentic Self and take your right to sit and shine with the stars above. You matter! Every fiber of you and every aspect of your life matters. Every thought you have, every word you speak, every second and moment you have here, how you look, feel, and sound, and how you want to express yourself matters. You are indeed one of a kind!

IN OUR MOTHER'S WOMB

"Truly I tell you, unless you change and become like little children,

you will never enter the kingdom of heaven."

- Mathew Chapter 18:3

No one remembers the precious and fragile phase of life we all had to pass through - our mothers' womb. This crucial and vulnerable stage in our lives lasts for about nine months. I'm sure we can all agree that we had nothing to do with this process; our conception, our growth formation until the day of our birth. It all happened outside of our control. This wonderful and magical process just took place, and then we arrived.

Imagine that at about four weeks, the embryo, a magic ball of cells, was carrying you and me, much like an acorn bearing the potential of a giant oak tree! All that growing, all that forming, all that branching out and offering protective shade and homes for animals and other creatures, improving the quality of the air we breathe by storing carbon dioxide and providing oxygen. All that potential in an acorn carried in that tiny seed, like every other expression of life here with its unique attributes, characteristics, and benefits, taking shape and form, journeying with an invisible and mystical hand that knew exactly where to place it.

This is a life process we all take for granted, and it is happening by itself, without any striving, trying, or pushing. It happened and is happening, yet we never really take the time to ponder what this means for our lives. At six weeks, our nose, mouth, and ears are slowly starting to take shape, features that allow us to smell all those beautiful aromas throughout history, taste, communicate with, and kiss. Our ears hear the most majestic sounds and beautiful music we are all privileged to listen to. And yet, we have nothing to do with forming these gifts. It is all happening by itself.

Our part is to float and trust life. It will take us every step of those formative phases we must go through. So how are these extraordinary magical processes happening consistently and flawlessly everywhere in the cosmos, every second of each day without our help, consistently and beautifully? While on the other side of the flip coin, life on earth has become one of competition, war, and strife?!

Mozart played the piano at the tender age of three, making his first composition at 5. Beethoven, at age 5, was already a masterful violinist. Kevin Chen from Canada was composing at age 6. My son, at age 8, asked for a guitar out of the blue, without any family members playing any instruments, and has since never put it down. So, if life formed us without any effort on our part, and gave us unique tastes, attributes, skills, and desires, why should we have to fight and compete? Why should we stress about our clothes, food, money, and material possessions when life itself is the treasure and already carries the image of the end result? An acorn doesn't say, "I want to be a pine tree," and an elephant doesn't say, "I want to be a cat." If we take a moment to reflect on our state as unborn children when we were tiny, soft, and vulnerable in our mothers' wombs, we might realize that life flowed and happened without interference, judgment, discrimination, or division. Yeshua put it this way:

The Parable of the Lost Coin

Or suppose a woman has ten silver coins and loses one.

Doesn't she light a lamp, sweep the house and search carefully

until she finds it? And when she finds it, she calls her friends and

neighbours together and says, 'Rejoice with me; I have found my lost coin.'

In the same way, I tell you, there is rejoicing in the Presence of the

Angels of God over one sinner who repents.

- Gospel of Luke 15:8-10

Here, Yeshua uses a story of a woman who loses a coin to make the same point. A coin carries an image or imprint of a person, just as we carry our True Nature within us. This True Nature is already present and can become lost or buried. By lighting the lamp through practices like meditation, contemplation, and clearing away hindrances, we can rediscover who we truly are. When we do, joy will return and overflow into our communities.

"Therefore I tell you, do not worry about your life, what you will eat

or drink, or about your body, what you wear. Is life more than food

and the body more than clothes?"

- Gospel of Matthew 6:25

FROM THE WOMB TO THE BREAST

Yet you are He who took me out of the womb;
You made me hope and trust when I was on my mother's breasts.
- Book of Psalms 22 v 9

From the womb of our mothers, we are soon held to their bosom, and our instincts guide us towards their nipple so that we can receive the goodness provided by milk. This milk provides us with the sustenance and building blocks necessary to grow. Even as newborns, we instinctively find the breast and begin suckling within minutes, just as quickly and essentially as breathing. We don't need a dress rehearsal or practice to navigate the nipple, as a newborn's innate knowledge guides them precisely in what to do.

What a beautiful metaphor and clue into the position we should take with our lives. We should trust and rest in the bosom of our trustworthy Source and receive spiritual food, wisdom, and direction so that we can grow not only as physical beings but as spiritual beings receiving nourishment for our souls. In our formative years, we all had an open, trusting heart with the ability to direct us to the exact place and time we needed to be. This force allows the natural flow of life to guide our tiny steps, a magical flow of Cosmic Intelligence that we have all experienced at different points in our lives. This same intelligence gives millions of monarch butterflies the ability to travel from their summer breeding grounds in North Eastern U.S. and Canada to their overwintering grounds in South-Western Mexico. We possess this intelligent Life Force within us, but we have to re-learn how to listen to it and trust it.

As human beings, we encounter all sorts of trials and tribulations as we journey through this ever-changing and, at times, demanding world we all live in. Learning to trust a higher state of awareness or consciousness is something we can learn from observing this wonderful creature, the monarch butterfly that does exactly that to survive. Can you imagine how dangerous the journey is for this tiny little butterfly that weighs less than half a gram and has a wingspan of about four inches? Such vulnerability, and yet it is so brave to endure such a demanding task for its short lifespan, trusting wholeheartedly in what it senses and knowing precisely what it has to do. Imagine being one of these little creatures telling your family and friends that you are about to embark on an epic journey through some of the most demanding terrain and weather conditions. Most would immediately demand that you stop, insisting it is too dangerous and that you would never make it. Logical, practical, caring advice, right?

Position yourself like a child resting on the heart and bosom of its mother and learn how to hear the sound of her heartbeat - not just any old heartbeat, but the unconditional loving heartbeat of a mother willing to lay down her life for her child. It is here that we learn to let go and trust in the sound of our own heart, whispering sacred truths. We are perfectly and wonderfully made as we are; we are whole, complete, and perfect as we arrived; and just as we are, we are the greatest gift to ourselves and to life, and should never be compromised.

I liken this part of our early life journey to the simple action of one disciple of Yeshua, when the beloved disciple named John leaned on Yeshua's chest, whom Yeshua loved. He rested in this intimate posture (Gospel of John 13:23-26), leaning upon the heart he had grown to know and love dearly, relaxing and listening to the very essence that he once felt from his loving mother. It is a compassionate love that profoundly emanates from a soul that whispers:

> Greater Love hath no man than this,
> that a man lay down his life for his friends.
> - Gospel of John 15 v 13

To lean upon your own heart requires a deep surrender to a life that causes our breath to breathe, our organs to form, and our mouths to find our mother's nipple, with the same confidence that the monarch butterfly demonstrates during its arduous journey. To know that our hearts carry the very substance of love that formed every cell in our body is to truly and unfalteringly understand that love can direct our steps, if we only rest as the beloved John rested on the chest of the Master Yeshua. This is the most valuable knowledge, priceless and sacred to the sensitive, and to those who dare to listen and wait for the indwelling presence to reveal itself.

Seek Him everywhere,

All is within His reach.

He knoweth all things.

Full of wisdom,

He determineth

What ought to be done,

He is our only recourse.

All powers are vested in Him.

He fulfilleth all our aspirations.

He is the Source of all our nourishment and vigour,

Intelligence and strength.

- Rig 1.145.1

Ask, and it will be given to you; seek, and you will find;

knock, and the door will be opened to you.

For everyone who asks receives; the one who seeks finds;

and to the one who knocks, the door will be opened.

- Gospel of Matthew 7 v 7-8

Your heart knows the way; run in that direction.

- Rumi

OUR ORIGINAL FACE

Before you entered the womb, arrived here on this planet, and took incarnation, have you ever wondered who you were before you were born? There is a well-known saying in Zen Buddhism, *'show me your Original Face, the face you had before your parents were born.'* It speaks of a true, authentic, unblemished, and pure Self without any of the constructs, past dramas, or judgements that we have all formed in ourselves. It speaks of a moment of endless, eternal, infinite, now Presence; a presence genuinely us at essence, fully awakened and whole; naked, empty of 'self', full heart, pure Light. But how does the Light see the Light? How does the naked know nakedness? Can the wind catch the wind? Can fire feel the fire? Can spirit see spirit? How can one see its own Presence? How can one see its own nakedness when it is naked? What if we are not meant to see ourselves with our "earthly" material eyes but rather to know ourselves first and, in knowing ourselves, eventually see ourselves?

Like clouds that often cover the sun and eventually move past, revealing the glory and beauty of the sun, we too have clouds that obscure our True Nature. And when those clouds are allowed to pass, as all energies eventually do under the Law of Impermanence, our True Light will surface as the sun rises each morning, radiating its True Essence. This means, ***"You are the light of this world"***. We are all made of this essence, this eternal Light that often gets covered and lost by the storms we face.

In the ***Gospel of John 8:58***, Yeshua was asked by some religious leaders if he was greater than their Father Abraham. Yeshua's response deeply shocked them: "Before ***Abraham was, I AM***." In fact, they picked up stones to throw at him because they could not bear to hear him speak with such authority about who he claimed to be. But in this response, Yeshua reveals a hidden treasure for understanding one's true originality and true authentic self. He unlocks the key to discovering who we are and where we came from.

Understanding that we are all extensions of the Eternal Light puts an absolute end to all the chasing, striving, searching, and dead religious activities that we, as human beings, engage in to try and reach somewhere.

This response, "***Before Abraham was, I AM***," should be the end of our search and the beginning of our rest here on planet Earth because it reveals that there is nowhere to get to, nothing to become, and nothing one can or should do to reach or become anything. This is the real **good news**, the gospel, and the reason the early followers of the Way were persecuted for almost 300 years. Yeshua reveals a powerful truth that had been buried and kept away from the masses: that we are carriers of the very substance, the image and likeness, the Presence and Light of the Eternal One. The One who is without form, the One who commanded that '*no graven images'* be made of Him because He is without condition, beyond description, beyond thoughts and words. We are all extensions of His very breath and nature. Based on the Lotus Sutra, Nichiren maintained that "*all living beings possess the Buddha nature*".

This fundamental truth reveals the very nature of our origins, the fibre and quintessence of what and who we are. It shows a limitless space of awareness that is luminous, expansive, and beyond conceptual fabrication; a place within all of us that is free from the constant movement and the noise of our thoughts; a place where we can find shelter, rest, and true comfort. The union of emptiness, the birth of clarity and radiant awareness become a lamp and guide to our feet. Another way to explain this is to say that Buddha Nature is something that we are, together with all beings, here, now, and always. It is something that we all carry but may not be aware of, as we often cling to false ideas of who we are or are made to feel at times that we are less, worthless, not good enough, not white enough, or any other false idea to which we have been exposed. This is why, when souls suddenly awaken to this beautiful truth of who they are, they are ready to risk everything for it, knowing that this path leads to liberation and freedom from suffering. When a wave suddenly feels and knows it is the ocean, or a soul knows it is one with all life, there is no separation. This is a liberating message that all great teachers revealed during their time and in their culture and tradition.

I hope you can feel this as a letter of love to you, my brother, sister, and friend. I am gently whispering and reminding you that you are not your bank balance, your material success, the car you drive, the house you own (or don't own), or how much you think you contribute to this material world. Instead, you are carrying the very substance of the Eternal One; you are the treasure of all treasures. The same essence and fragrance of your presence are in the Awakened One, the Light of this world, and the Salt of the earth. We are that!

Maybe no one has ever told you or reminded you of this before, but you feel it deep within, without a reference. But I am here to remind you, just as Brother Sun reminds you, Sister Moon, and all the beautiful trees and stars at night. You are indeed woven into the vast tapestry of the Universe, as unique as every setting of the sun, as authentic as every season we all experience, and without you, this whole would not be whole! Let these words echo in your heart: **'It is finished.'"**

It is done. You are perfect just as you are. There is no more need to try, my friend, no need to try to become anything or to fit in or please anyone. You are simply perfect as you are. No more need to work it all out in the dimension of your limited, overactive thinking mind. Instead, sink and surrender, fall into the here and now, without trying, fully accepting that you are **it**, you really are **IT**! There is nothing more to add or take away, change or transform. The chase is over, and surrendering with full acceptance is the way. What a relief! What a rest for your journeyed soul. What a massive weight off your shoulders! You don't have to do anything more!

You, my dear friend, are sitting, sleeping, walking, and working in the *result*. You are the result, and your journey of sinking into this has begun. Well done! You have come this far and were meant to read this love letter. You were led to this point, and I rejoice with you! So, take a moment and feel deep gratitude for your rest, for what your precious heart and mind are feeling right now. You are deeply loved by The All.

BEYOND THE MIND

With the increasing demands on all our lives and the busy timetables that fit these demands, few people have the time and space to ask, 'Is there anything beyond the dimension of thoughts or feelings? Is there something beyond this body and this thinking mind?' There is. And when you discover it, it will change everything in your life. Only when you discover this unique part of yourself will you experience liberty and freedom from the shadows, scars, and impressions of your past.

When the Yaoshan was sitting, a monk asked him, "What do you do when you sit?" Yaoshan replied, "I think of not thinking." The monk asked, "How do you think of not thinking?" Yaoshan said, "Beyond thinking."

The above is a dialogue between a Chinese Zen Master, Yaoshan Weiyan, and one of his students. It isn't that Yaoshan doesn't think, but rather that he doesn't get pulled, influenced, or moved by thoughts. For it is the function of the mind to think, but a 'thinking' that is immersed and one with pure, clear Awareness radiating through it, paused and in a state of calm-abiding readiness, and when called into action, will flow naturally without any obstructions. So very much like a clear, slow-moving stream without any bubbles coming to the surface, free from the constant jumping from one thing to the next: a mind that is not grasping nor attached to positive or negative outcomes or stories, but one that is formless and free from form, ideas, beliefs, and sense pleasures, and can immediately fit into whatever space presents itself and yet, leave without a trace, without any internal effect or impression upon it.

When we turn our awareness and attention inward and learn to sit in the streams of clear abiding is-ness, a word I'm using to describe that which always was, is, and is to come. When all our notions about external, internal, negative, and positive dissolve, our minds form a union and connect with the whole. The abiding practice of this eventually dissolves the internal formations and patterns we have trained ourselves in. By abiding in this stillness, we stop feeding the very nature of these constructs, preventing them from the fuel they require to live, form, and grow into mental constructs and even form into bad habits. This calm-abiding eventually allows us to experience this formless or unattached mind.

There is one significant factor that needs to be considered, and that is emptying our cups. Without letting go of the things we are clinging to, the ideas we are attached to, can there ever be an experience beyond our thoughts. For the nature of thoughts, if we cling to them, they become rigid and fixed. Fixed in their patterns, they are unable to move and change when the moment requires us to move. And it is this grasping and holding on that leads to suffering. Suffering because we cannot deal with the moment's reality, unable to let go and flow with the absolute truth. What is beyond your worries, fears, stresses, tension, and anxiety, if I asked you?

You wouldn't be able to answer until everything ceases to exist, and you genuinely experience it. But if I asked you, "Why are you afraid? Why are you worried? Why are you anxious?" Upon quick reflection, you could give me a very detailed description. However, that is because you are dealing with the dimension of thoughts. "I am worried because I think this is going to happen, or that is going to happen, and I am afraid." We train ourselves to do this very well from a very young age. We all know that a vast amount of what we think about daily is entirely nonsense and a massive waste of time and energy. Yet, we believe it's quite normal when it's addictive and harmful. By teaching people to grip and hold on to ideas, outcomes, views, or religious beliefs, we're teaching our once-clear minds to grasp, hold on, become attached, and then become defensive of the things we cling to. But in reality, we will all lose everything one day. We will lose our loved ones, our close friends, our wealth, our properties, our hair, our strength, and eventually, our bodies.

We are not 'accumulating' beings. We are born with a small measure of time. Our life here is but a mere vapor. Like a flash of lightning, we come and we will go. So why grasp? Why hold on? Why become fixed and rigid when life and reality constantly change and move from one to the next? Wouldn't it be wiser to live wholeheartedly in life itself, free, unattached, fully present, and with an understanding of the Law of Impermanence?

If we consider the Cosmos, the Universe, and Space, we can observe that they are in constant motion due to various forces of existence - gravitational, electromagnetic, and nuclear - causing continuous movement in all directions, here and now. Despite this constant motion, nothing is grasping or fixed, yet there is order and sometimes chaos, as everything is constantly changing and renewing. Nothing is static. However, within this constant motion, movement, change, and renewal, there is a Stillness that is ever-present everywhere and at all times, here and now, forever moving to the next.

Think about all the billions of tiny creatures beneath the soil and beneath the ocean, constantly in motion, changing and renewing. And within it all, there is an invisible, cementing Stillness that glues everything together. We can become aware of this Stillness, merge with it, and flow with its currents rather than against them, giving this Presence full permission to be within and without us. How amazing, beautiful, and majestic is life.

PRESENCE, NOT PERSON

For years, I was told, instructed, and motivated by nearly everyone I knew to become *'someone'* - a person that needed to be respected. I was told that I needed to be 'smart' to be accepted by society, to survive in this world, and make something of my life. I was told that I needed to improve in everything I did, like an actor playing a role, constantly striving to be better. This was the mantra that echoed in every institution and organization on earth, especially in a world of constant competition, expansion, and the pursuit of material success. Souls lose themselves in the pursuit of becoming something outside themselves, outside the present moment. We adopt this false ideology and soon begin the chase to become wealthier, more powerful, more acceptable, more charming, and more talented, living in ignorance of our true beautiful Presence. We sell out and prostitute ourselves just to live, when the truth is that life is happening by itself. We chase a dream, an illusion, a construct that we make up of ourselves from the dimension of our thoughts, usually motivated by our fears. These thoughts become agreements that we painfully follow, believing they will offer some form of joy and deep contentment until we discover they are empty and then feel we are missing something. Our consumer-driven world does not help, constantly bombarding us with messages of 'you need more of this', 'the next one up', or 'the latest design', making souls feel inadequate and worthless, always seeking and wanting to become more, but never feeling like we are *'getting there'*. However, there is nowhere to get to.

This dangerous trap starts when we believe that who we are is not enough. It is the leading cause of why souls lose themselves to everything other than their authentic, whole, and unique Presence. Imagine if one day, the sun says, 'I don't feel that what I am is good enough, so from today, I am going to become like the moon.' What a disaster that would be! But it doesn't happen in nature, so it should not happen to our true nature either.

Replacing our authentic Presence in exchange for another idea of who we are, because we think it will improve us, prevent rejection, help us become wealthier and more powerful, or more accepted in a particular group, is a sure way to spiral into further rejection and disappointment. The more we adopt another version of ourselves, the more we reject our true selves, and the more we do this, the more we will feel as though we are never enough. Self-rejection is a form of self-sabotage, convincing ourselves that who we are doesn't fit the benchmark. Only when a soul accepts that every fibre of who they are is perfect, will they find true and lasting peace.

A beautiful story in the Buddhist scriptures provides insight into this matter. It is the story of an individual named Aṅgulimāla and his encounter with the Buddha, which I will elaborate on to highlight my point. The story goes like this:

One day, after the Buddha had finished eating, he left the monastery where he was staying and walked slowly and quietly towards a great forest. When people saw him heading towards the forest, they warned him that he was approaching the dreaded and most feared Aṅgulimāla, a killer who caused many to flee their homes.

The name Aṅgulimāla means "*garland of fingers*," which refers to the necklace he had made from the fingers of his victims whom he had killed. This powerful and athletic serial killer was once a student and a son, but he suddenly transformed into a killing machine. Many say he was angered by seeing weaker members of society being bullied, and having witnessed his parents being publicly humiliated. He adopted a self-fulfilling idea of himself, hoping to gain respect through fear and force. However, Aṅgulimāla soon became isolated and deeply lonely, clinging to the mercy of his troubled mind and wandering around with a deep feeling of self-rejection. This led to self-hatred, causing suffering not only to himself but also to all those around him.

As the Buddha approached his dwelling, Aṅgulimāla grabbed his weapons and ran out, intending to take on his next victim, unbeknownst to him that it would be the Buddha. Expecting to catch him quickly, the Buddha walked mindfully with every step, as if kissing the Earth. Aṅgulimāla was unable to reach him, and the more he strained to catch him, the deeper his struggle became. Eventually, Aṅgulimāla grew exhausted, increasingly angry with every attempt to capture the Buddha. Then, he screamed, "STOP!!" The Buddha turned around unhurriedly and peacefully responded, saying, "I have stopped, but you haven't."

Aṅgulimāla was struck by these words. He instantly saw all the false agreements he had made with himself and the resounding rejection of his true nature as he looked upon the face of the one who had fully awakened. It was as though he was looking at a mirror and saw his own Buddha nature. That was when he stopped, dropped, gave up, and let go of the chase. The burden he had been carrying all those years had ended abruptly.

When you encounter someone who is living in their true nature, it's like looking into a mirror that reflects who you truly are. You don't need to see the Buddha or Christ physically present to recognize your own potential, as they have already turned towards our circumstances, revealing what we possess inside. The key is to stop and accept that we are already that, and give ourselves time and space to fully embrace this realization. With patience and practice, we can enter into a state of rest and complete peace with ourselves and others.

Aṅgulimāla, once a feared murderer, experienced this transformation when he encountered the Buddha. He followed the Buddha, became a monk, and completely transformed his life and community.

I am deeply grateful to the Buddha and all those who have walked the earth, for reminding us that what we are is enough, and that our presence here on earth is the only real gift and treasure worth pursuing. May we all awaken to the knowledge of this truth and, like Aṅgulimāla, prevent the wheels from spinning further away from who we really are.

WE ARE HERE

Be still and know that I AM
- Book of Psalms 46:10

Much has been said and written about living and being in the present moment. Yet, many people are still consumed by their past, anxious about their future, or stuck in bitterness, anger, unforgiveness, or pride. Some are fortunate to find refuge, but unfortunately, the majority continue to suffer in the constant cycle of these patterns with little or no help. Nowadays, being mindful has become a fashionable word, but it is a concept that needs to be explored to be truly understood. Otherwise, it may become just another passing trend that fades over time.

How can we become mindful and remain fully aware when we live in a society glued to our smartphones, chat groups, social media, and all the other latest gadgets that pull us in? How can we walk mindfully when most people have become reliant on these appliances? I understand that in today's world, most people rely on these platforms. While they have their benefits from both social and business perspectives, they should never replace your peace, consume your time, or cause worry or distress.

Recent studies in the US and Europe have shown that increased use of social media causes delayed sleep and even sleep loss. It also enhances the chances of depression, memory loss, and anxiety. These findings indicate that filling our minds constantly with more and more information only causes people to feel overwhelmed, less able to concentrate, and tired. There is a limit to what we can take in, and balance is essential to managing all these things. While we encourage people to be more mindful and be present in the moment, we have simultaneously created a global culture suffering from the harmful effects of information overload.

How can the mind settle to enjoy the magic and gift of the present moment when it is constantly searching, seeking, and dreaming of something better? And what happens to the mind that doesn't get what it wants? It becomes increasingly frustrated, agitated, and angry and will seek other desires and pleasures to quench its fires. It's challenging to live in the here and now, enjoy the moment, and appreciate beauty with all these triggers. The truth is that you can't do it all the time, and you may have fleeting moments, but then you will return to the same old spinning patterns and wheels. While those fortunate to be youthful may be able to handle the demands better, as the cycle and seasons pass, we all become weaker.

Life exists only in the present moment, and nowhere else. This is not something to grasp or debate about but to accept and embrace. Once we do, our energies will begin to harmonize and settle into the flow of life, and life will no longer become such an effort. However, before this can happen, there has to be a return to zero, an emptying. By emptying, I don't mean kissing your brains goodbye, but rather returning to clear, transparent light so that you can discern with razor-sharp awareness and insight. I say this because emptiness has been wrongly used and misunderstood when, in fact, emptiness is everywhere. You may have a significant title, a hugely important job with a large salary, a house, and a car or two. But the reality is that it is all empty space - 99.999999% of beautiful empty space.

A well-known Professor once went to visit a Zen Master. As the Master served tea, the Professor began to describe his Zen ideas from all the books he had read, all the information he had gathered online, and the stories he had picked up along his travels. The Zen Master remained quiet and very still, only pouring the tea while listening to the vast amount of information coming from the Professor's mouth. As he continued pouring out information, the Zen Master continued pouring tea. Soon, the cup was overflowing and spilling onto the tray, the table, and the floor until the Professor could no longer stand it. "Stop!" he said. "Can't you see the cup is full and spilling everywhere?" The Zen Master replied, "I am only mirroring you," followed by, "How can I show you Zen unless you first empty your cup?"

This Zen parable is a good depiction of how filling oneself with much information, then clinging onto the idea that that information is true insight, robs us of the here and now. The first step to entering the present moment is **listening**; for there to be listening, there must be emptying, becoming silent and still. The moment's essence can be found in Stillness, empty of any grasping, a humble space between here and now with nothing in-between.

CONTEMPLATION & REFLECTION

Before I Was, Presence
Presence, Before I Was

Please find a warm and comfortable place to sit, with your spine nice and straight. Allow your heart to be filled with immense gratitude, as though it is being filled with the warm, loving rays of the sun slowly embracing you. Become conscious of the sacred in and out breath, noticing that it is breathing you effortlessly. Life is living through and for you. No action is required as you contemplate this poem from my heart to yours:

You are light, you always were, and you will always be.
You may have forgotten a little.
Okay, return and feel the light burn.
This light is your treasure,
without any pressure,
without measure.
For how long? Forever.
This light that is you is awake,
fully aware, fully to share.
Where? Everywhere.
This light restores,
like an embracing seashore.
It heals as the ego peels. It warms your heart,
even when it feels like falling apart.
This light points to the path
And reveals the way,
even when you don't pray.
Why?
Because light lights up,
wherever it goes.
The darkness doesn't comprehend it,
it only feels its brightness
and then it's too late.
The light is your Source, of course.
It's your bravery,

your courage,
your bright individual expression,
your real possession.
Above all else, the light is your truth,
in every situation.
Your honesty is your only policy.

CHAPTER 2

IT BREATHED US

If we observe our bodies, we will soon discover that we have much in common with our planet. Not just the fact that we are made of the same elements, primarily made up of water, sharing around the same percentage, as we have veins and arteries moving blood around our bodies. Similarly, rivers and streams move and carry water in and around our planet, providing life to all. So, we can say that the clay of the earth and we have a natural resemblance; thus, the words "from dust to dust" are birthed.

But let's go deeper. What is giving life to this dust? Or, to be more specific, these elements? And who creates the program with precise instructions to perform every task? The kidneys remove waste, the heart moves blood throughout the body, the lungs pass oxygen into the bloodstream, and the brain is the main control centre of thinking, feeling, and gathering, remembering, seeing, hearing, and breathing. All of these chemicals come together; trillions of cells repairing and rebuilding; the brain with the ability to hold, gather and arrange vast amounts of information; the heart with the ability to pump and beat around 100,000 times a day; the eyes with the ability to distinguish up to one million color surfaces and take in more information than the biggest and best computer system. Your unique fingerprints confirm that there is only one unique You on the entire planet! What creative and brilliant energy flows suddenly, miraculously arranging and organizing all these vast amounts of complex information to work simultaneously here, now and everywhere? WOW! What a miracle! And it is all happening without us, without anything that you or I have done or are doing. All we are doing is enjoying the food and water provided freely.

So, on close examination, peeling fruit, putting the fruit in our mouths, and moving our jaws to chew, and even then, digestion is already happening by itself as the salivary glands are forming saliva, helping the food to travel through easier. Once again, it is happening to us and for us.

Life on every level is a gift, mysteriously happening and serving our every moment here. In Middle Eastern texts, it is written that, The All breathed life into us. And in the book of *Ecclesiastes 12:7*, the text goes on to say that at the point of death, the same breath returns to the Source.

Then shall the dust return to the earth as it was:
And the spirit shall return unto God who gave it.
- Ecclesiastes 12:7

The primordial, clear, untainted light that gives life to all, the same source that provides us with the ability to breathe, is, in truth, breathing us. So every breath we take is happening, and when we realize that every breath is the very spiritual essence of The All, we can say that the Spirit of God is giving us life with its sheer energy flowing through us. Therefore, our life becomes an extension of His life, our breath becomes His breath, or Thy Breath.

> For in him we live, and move, and have our being.
> - Book of Acts 17:28

All life, movement and beings are in union with the One, yet not all life is in communion with the One. And this is the true calling and path that leads to perfect peace, as Yeshua beautifully expressed:

> And this is life eternal, that they might know Thee
> - Gospel of John 17:3

We are designed and created to walk in union and communion with The All, allowing the very life and power to co-exist with us here on earth in an intimate friendship. It is all happening in Him, through Him, and because of Him. Our deepest desire is to awaken to this knowledge and understanding. But it starts when we allow the very breath, the same spirit, the very life of The All to move within us. For that to happen, we need to soften and allow space and emptiness to exist within, giving the breath the freedom, room, and access to move as it wants. We are to gently listen, in a mode of stillness, to the quiet ocean, rising and falling until the currents become as silent as the night sky in the desert. Here, you will begin to feel that it is all breathing you, and the "you" and "I" that we often think exist separately from The All will slowly dissolve into emptiness. When this starts to happen, the joy and peace you will experience will be like one that surpasses all understanding. Even now, as you have been led to these pages, it is breathing you, and it is all happening without effort, as it always was. So again, the call to let go and allow the breath to breathe and life to flow is whispering, "*Allow* me to breathe, and your true life will appear."

> In the beginning
>
> there was neither existence
>
> nor non-existence,

neither sky nor beyond.

That One breathed, without breath,

by His own breathless power.

The first-born was the Creative Will,

the Primordial seed of the mind.

All else followed.

The sages, searching for the truth

within themselves,

discovered the eternal bond

between the seen and the unseen.

This bond was an endless line stretched

across the heavens.

What was above?

Was below?

Primal seeds were sprouting

Mighty forces were moving

Pulsation from below

Pure energy above.

Who here knows? Who can say for sure?

When it began, and from where it came - this creation?

The gods came afterwards, so who really knows?

From where this creation came,

By what means was it formed,

Only He who watches from the highest knows

Or perhaps even He does not know!

- Rig Veda, Book X 129

THE SACRED BREATH

Why look for God?... Look for the one looking for God... but then why look at all?
He is not lost... He is right here... Closer than our very breath!

\- Rumi

Rumi once breathed these inspired words. Indeed, what is closer than our breath, and what is the force that moves it? Furthermore, what gives this force the energy to move with its unique rhythm? We all know that this life force energy exists, yet we cannot see it. We often feel its magical pulses in moments of poetry, art, music, and nature, profoundly moving us, yet we cannot quite describe it. It is like trying to fathom the unfathomable.

In the classic text, the Tao Te Ching, it is described this way:

The Tao (Way) that can be told of is not the eternal Tao (Way)

It cannot be explained, put in a box, or even named. If we define it, then it cannot be it. This, of course, is a huge stumbling block to our minds, which desperately want to grasp onto things and put them into a category, to place them in a fitting division or class.

In all the ancient texts, the breath and the sacred have always been linked, mainly because the breath is the most intimate sensation we feel and experience, the closest thing to both life and death. It is pure, undefiled, and untarnished because we cannot grab or change it. It is there in all of us, happening so mystically without any effort. And because there is nothing more to do, it seems hard to grasp as everything we have been taught from a young age is the complete opposite. No effort is required here, no work is needed, and as long as you think there is, you will keep missing the Sacred Breath. This happens only when we acknowledge and accept that we are being breathed, we are energized, we are being moved, we are being held, and we are being breathed upon.

Yeshua, in the *Gospel of John 20:22*, says that He *(Yeshua)* breathed upon his disciples saying, ***"Receive the Holy Spirit"***, and another more accurate translation, ***"Receive the Spirit of Holiness"***. In this inspired moment, the Sacred Breath that flowed through Yeshua was untarnished, without blemish, *and Holy*. Holy because it came from the Source; pure, whole and deeply sacred. It is here that Yeshua reveals and imparts a vital key to his beloved disciples.

The Breath, the **Sacred Breath**, is the key to forming an intimate union with the Source. It is the gateway and path into the Holy of Holies, the most secret place within you and me. There is nothing else for us to do, as there was nothing else required for the disciples to do other than receive the knowledge and understanding that the Sacred Breath was breathing through their veins. The knowledge and understanding that this Sacred Breath is the heartbeat of God living in and through us. The One we are searching for has been searching for us all this time. Only it was so close and intimate that we easily missed it.

Yeshua would often say things like, "The Spirit gives life, the flesh counts for nothing. The words I have spoken to you, they are full of spirit and life" (*Gospel of John 6:63*). It was his complete surrender and reliance on that which gives life, the Source, rather than relying on his own efforts. This was the secret to his demonstrated power. And this was the fundamental truth he was trying to impart to his students and all who would follow this Way.

You only have to observe his students after they realize the Sacred Breath or the Holy Spirit to see its impact on their lives. They were filled with power, authority, peace, and stability and did the same acts as their Master. As a result, they caused a colossal awakening, shaking the entire Roman Empire.

And they were filled with the Holy Spirit and began to speak in

other languages, as the Holy Spirit gave them this ability.

-   Book of Acts 2:2

In the **Gospel of John 15:26**, Yeshua describes the Holy Spirit as the *Helper* and *Comforter*, a very personal friend who endowed his followers with help to strengthen them in times of trouble, a disclosure of truth and wisdom, opening a way where there seems to be no way. This Spirit is the force and Source that gives life to the micro and the macro; it's the same Source that causes all movement.

Yeshua said: If they say to you: Whence have you come? Say to them: We have come from the light, the place where the light came into being of itself.

It [established itself], and it revealed itself in their image.

If they say to you: Who are you? say: We are his sons, and we are the elect of

the living Father. If they ask you: What is the sign of your Father in you?

Say to them: It is movement and rest.

- Gospel of Thomas 50:1-2

The idea that "life is mine" and that "I" and "me" exists outside this Force is what moves us away from sensing the Presence and power of the Sacred Breath. But the moment we let go of the "me, myself and I" is when we begin to feel and experience the power and covering blanket of the Holy Spirit.

Do you know that your bodies are temples of the Holy Spirit,

who is in you, whom you have received from God?

- 1 Corinthians 6:19

You are not your own. We are not our own. Our lives do not belong to us, nor have we come by anything we have done. Yes, we manage and organise our lives, but we don't own them, nor are we the Source of our lives. So, connecting to the Sacred Breath, the Holy Breath, with the understanding that *It* is breathing you and moving you, is the beginning of a beautiful and intimate loving friendship you can enjoy here on earth. Opening this pathway allows the Sacred One to finally reveal Himself to you as a close and personal friend. One who will always be by your side, covering you with wings of Love, energising you with fresh streams of power, leading you into truth and reality, whispering words of encouragement, setting you free with joy and peace in your heart. Another way of understanding this is that there is actual *Presence* wherever mindfulness is. Furthermore, letting go of the "I" or "my" reality brings us to the Sacred Presence that both Yeshua and the Buddha lived from and always pointed to.

But the fruit of the Spirit is Love, joy, peace, longsuffering, gentleness,

goodness, faith, meekness, temperance: against such, there is no law.

- Galatians 5:22-23

The hallmarks of a soul who comes into rest and understands that letting go of the "my life", that the "Our" life appears before them. But first, there is the receiving, just as the students of the Buddha had to learn by sitting in stillness until only Stillness is present. But this is only the beginning. How blessed are we, who discover this inner treasure now, in this life, and have this gift of opportunity to swim in the eternal currents of the vast ocean we call Eternal Life?

Before you turn to the next page, take a moment to inhale and exhale, but this time, let your breath flow naturally and move your body as it wishes. Allow your breath to move as it wants. Remember that you are the temple, the actual dwelling place of this peaceful Presence. Simply receive this blessing wherever you are, at whatever stage you have reached, and let the Sacred Breath move through you.

Not Christian or Jew or Muslim, not Hindu, Buddhist, Sufi or Zen.

Not any religion or cultural system.

I am not from the East or the West,

not out of the ocean or up from the ground,

not natural or ethereal, not composed of elements at all.

I do not exist, am not an entity in this world or in the next,

did not descend from Adam or Eve or any origin story.

My place is placeless, a trace of the traceless.

Neither body nor soul.

I belong to the beloved and have seen the two worlds as

one and that one call to and know, first, last, outer, inner,

only that breath-breathing human being.

- Rumi

OUR WORTH, OUR UNIQUENESS

Albert Einstein once said, "Everybody is a genius. But if you judge a fish by its ability to climb a tree, it will live its whole life believing it is stupid." Everyone is a genius because no two people are the same. Even identical twins who grew up with the same genes and nurturing parents, and in the same environment, turn out to be different and have their own way of expressing life. This uniqueness is what we call individual personalities. No two brains are precisely the same or wired the same, so no two eyes could ever see the same, nor two ears ever hear the same. We all arrived here with our own exceptional and unique brand, making us diverse. Every living creature on Earth has a signature with its brand of uniqueness.

Despite our differences, we are all connected and able to think, reason, make choices, and exercise our free will. This connects and binds us together as humankind. We also share everyday needs for food, warmth, shelter, clothes, friends, music, and art. Yet, no two people are identical. Each individual is genuinely one of a kind, and this is the first of many treasures that every soul has to ponder to know its worth deeply.

Every soul born on Earth should be celebrated, cherished, and loved for who they are and their unique way of being and expressing, no matter how different that expression may be. That is why every soul needs space to be and grow in how they feel deep within. The word "feel" is used because children feel everything without the full ability to express those feelings. When they are not given space to be who they feel deep within, they may feel rejected and later find it difficult to find a place they can call "home".

Every soul needs this space and a carpet of love to make mistakes. When they do, their individual life and expression will spring forth, and they will radiate with worth and value. We must understand that we are all here with different expressions of intelligence, weaknesses, and strengths. Some have arrived as poets, while others come as scientists, athletes, musicians, or politicians, and some have a love for animals and the plant kingdom.

As Einstein said, *"If we judged a fish by its ability to climb a tree, it would believe it was stupid all its life."* Recognising and acknowledging the natural expression of intelligence in an individual without judgement or placing high and low, we can begin to function and serve the whole. It's very similar to our bodies, we have organs with unique and individual functions, yet all serve the same purpose. We don't say that the heart has far more worth than the lungs or the lungs far more than kidneys or liver. We don't esteem one higher or lower, right? Each one is serving life. *Our* life.

If I asked to buy your right eye, right ear, or left lung, what price would you quote me?" You wouldn't because no amount of money could buy the gift of your precious life. This is why every fibre of you, every living cell in your anatomy, is so sacred. Nowadays, there are many schools of thought, groups, and countless self-help books, all trying to change or transform everyone rather than seeing and affirming the beauty we all already possess. It is no wonder most people walk around with a sense of not being enough, always reaching out to improve or perfect themselves. If you observe this closely enough, you'll realize that we're hacking away at our actual worth and value, doing what Einstein warned against.

These subtle put-downs can be as simple as "you are good but not great", "pretty but not beautiful", "grade B but not quite an A", or "you sound good but not quite like Michael Jackson". These responses or subtle gestures (even at the thought level) can make people feel that they are never good enough, rejected, or unwanted. They may even develop a sense of shame and unworthiness, striving for perfection and constantly comparing themselves with others. How can one ever celebrate their life like this? How can one feel a deep sense of value and worth or ever have feelings of gratitude if they have never been told they are perfect, unique, and sacred just as they are?

Let me tell you, your uniqueness in life *is* your very gift to life itself. So, I want you to feel these words and stop comparing yourself to others. Stop always trying to please people, and stop selling yourself short. You don't need to apologise to anyone for who you are or how you think, speak or see the world. Just *as you are* is perfect; don't let anyone tell you otherwise!

Once, there was a young and rugged shepherd boy who was not deemed worthy enough by his father. However, one day, a prophet named Samuel recognized the young boy's potential and anointed him with oil, knowing he would one day become a king. This young boy was none other than King David, who went on to become famous for slaying Goliath. Despite spending most of his time alone with the sheep in the field, he knew himself and the source of his being. He was also a musician who wrote many songs, later compiled as the Book of Psalms.

David's beautiful words in one of his songs speak of the wonderful truth that the soul who comes into rest and understands the importance of letting go of "my life" can experience the "Our" life. However, first, one must learn to receive, just as the Buddha's students had to learn by sitting in *stillness* until only stillness was present. This is only the beginning, and how blessed are we to discover this inner treasure and have the gift of the opportunity to swim in the eternal currents of the vast ocean we call eternal life in this life.

Before you turn to the next page, take a deep breath in and out. But this time, allow the natural flow of your breath to guide and move you as it wills. Give your breath permission to move freely. Remember that you are the temple, the actual dwelling place of this peaceful presence. Receive this blessing wherever you are and at whatever station you have arrived, and allow the sacred breath to breathe through you.

For You formed my inward parts;

You covered me in my mother's womb.

I will praise You, for I am fearfully *and* wonderfully made;

Marvellous are Your works,

And *that* my soul knows very well.

My frame was not hidden from You,

When I was made in secret,

And skillfully wrought in the lowest parts of the earth.

Your eyes saw my substance, being yet unformed.

And in Your book, they all were written,

The days fashioned for me,

When *as yet there were* none of them.

- Book of Psalms 139:13-16

Ponder those words long enough to see why we are majestically and magically different. A lot of thought, imagination, and creativity has gone into our making. The trillion cells that started as one carry all the necessary information within that one seed. The brain controls our every move, while our eyelids protect our eyes and act like windshields. Our fingerprints were formed during the first three months of pregnancy. These details were accurately measured, calculated, and woven together with the exact information that makes each creation its own kind.

Contemplate deeply on this until you discover a personal touch in the making of every creature, as expressed through King David's words, "fearfully and wonderfully made". It is as though reminding us all to pause and wonder how deeply personal our Maker was when designing us. We are different, unique, and special, like the sun, the moon, and every star, insect, cell, or creature, as we have come forth from a Brilliant Mind. This Mind is original, imaginative, and creative, beyond anything we could ever grasp or fathom. And in this contemplation and pause, every soul will find rest, refuge, and true value.

We are all, indeed, fearfully and wonderfully made. We can remain quietly confident with the sun, the moon, the stars, the trees, and all our neighbours, rejoicing together as all creation rejoices, abiding in this great Love and knowing that we carry the very image, nature, and signature of the One Mind that has thought about every micro detail of His creation. We can sit and rest in this. Let there be light, and suddenly you came forth. How lucky we all are to have you, my brother and my sister. How fortunate we are!

THE SACRED MIRROR

Love is a mirror. In it you see nothing except your reflection.

You see nothing except your real face.

- Rumi

When Yeshua incarnated on Earth, he said and did some things that caused the authorities of his time to want him completely removed from the face of the planet. Often accused of making false claims about himself or the teachings he was giving to the multitude, other times it was because of the power he demonstrated when healing the sick, delivering those who were possessed by demons, and even raising Lazarus from the dead. These authorities felt completely threatened by this one man, his theology, and his religious system. They despised him passionately and wanted him dead, often attempting to stone him. One leading cause of this hatred eventually drove these religious leaders to hand him over to the Romans and have him crucified. But why would they hate such a man who healed the sick, you may ask? Because he claimed to be "one with God, His Father." This claim was seen as blasphemous, the worst kind of claim that a person can make in their eyes. The *Gospel of John 10:33* says (religious leaders speaking to Yeshua), *"We are not stoning you for any good work, but for blasphemy, because you, a mere man, claim to be God."*

In the *Gospel of John 14:8-11*, Philip *(a disciple)* said to Him, *"Lord, show us the Father, and it is enough for us"* Yeshua responds by saying, *"have I been with you so long, and you still do not know me, Philip? Whoever has seen me has seen the Father. How can you say, show us the Father? Do you not believe that I am in Father and the Father is in me? The word that I say to you, I do not speak on my own authority, but the Father who dwells in me does his works. Believe me that I am in the Father and the Father is in me, or else believe of the works themselves."*

Philip wasn't just any old student or disciple of Yeshua; he was one of the Twelve Apostles and would have spent years, many months, days, and hours in the company of their Master. And yet, this passage asks a straightforward and essential question that brings about a response revealing Yeshua's connection, life, and purpose. Notice how Philip asks Him to show them the Father, not if Yeshua was the Father. He could have asked him, "Are you God?" but instead he asked, "Show us the Father."

The question alone reveals that the disciple knew that Yeshua had access to the Source of Life, perhaps through the power and demonstrations that Yeshua did and that He often spoke of. Yet, Philip needed to learn how to access it himself. He knew there was a connection, a link, a union between Yeshua and the Father, with the power that ran through the very veins of Yeshua, but Philip and possibly all the other disciples still couldn't comprehend it and needed to see more evidence.

In *Genesis 1:27*, it is written that God made man in His image and likeness. Philip would have already known and read this text. There, right in front of him, was the very image and likeness, the "express" image and likeness of God, conversing with him and confirming that we all carry the image of our Creator. We are reflections of His light and presence and have the original likeness waiting to shine through us. How much more proof do we need to see? How long will it take for us to accept this truth about ourselves? Yeshua's response, *"have I been with you so long, and you still don't know who I am? I am in the Father, and the Father is in me; if you don't believe in that, then believe by my actions themselves."* This is one of the most important texts ever written because it reveals a hidden secret about who we are, where we come from, and what we have access to. In his reply, Jesus says something beautiful: 'I am in the Father, and the Father is in me.' He doesn't claim to be the Father, but he reveals that he is in a constant state of union, harmony, and oneness with the Father. Through this intimate relationship, he was able to do everything he did. This is why he said, *"I do not speak on my own authority, but the Father who dwells in me does his works."* In other words, Yeshua lived his life without any interference. Zero.

Yeshua had surrendered to the will of God and yielded to the path of divine and unconditional love, allowing a life force of healing to spring forth and help multitudes of souls. This way of life, with zero interference, is far more essential than arguing or disputing whether Yeshua was the Father, an Avatar, the second Adam, a Prophet, or God Himself. In the Gospel of John, the beloved disciple of Yeshua writes:

In the beginning, was the Word, and the Word was with God, and the Word was God. The same was in the beginning with God. All things were made by him;

and without him was not anything made that was made.

In him was life; and the life was the Light of men.

And the light shineth in darkness;

and the darkness comprehended it not.

– John 1:1-5

For centuries, if not millennia, people have wasted precious time debating whether Yeshua was God or just a Prophet, or whether the Buddha was an Avatar or a God, and so on about other enlightened beings. But the truth is, it doesn't change anything. So let God be God, Christ be Christ, and the Buddha be the Buddha... let it be. When Yeshua walked the earth, he said, *"I was naked, and you clothed me; I was sick, and you visited me; I was in prison, and you came to me. Truly, I say to you, as you did it to the least of these, my brothers, you did it to me."* (*Gospel of Matthew 25:36*).

He wasn't saying he was naked, sick, or in prison; he was expressing how much he was one with all human beings and that if any soul was suffering, he was suffering with them. He was also affirming the profound connection we have with one another, as well as with him, and how we are all carriers of the very nature of God, expressions of the One. Being one with the Source means being one with all that came from the Source.
This message of oneness was a profound truth that Yeshua courageously demonstrated throughout his ministry. If we can realize this and walk in it, then we too can enjoy a face-to-face encounter with the eternal radiant Presence and have a deep and intimate friendship with Him, just as Yeshua did.

One of Yeshua's most intimate and profound prayers is written in the *Gospel of John 17:3,* where he says:

"And this is eternal life, that they may know You, the only true God."

This was Yeshua's last prayer, desiring that all those who dared to follow his example might come into eternal life and know God. Nowhere in his prayers did he ever encourage his disciples to just 'recite prayers' or 'just sit in contemplation or meditation,' and he didn't even talk about saying 'mantras.' Here, it is clear that his deepest desire and prayer was for his disciples and all those who would follow to come to KNOW the one true God, the One whom Yeshua called his *'Father,'* literally speaking of an intimate, loving relationship.

The Son is the radiance of God's glory and the exact representation of His Being.

–   Hebrews 1:3

This text refers to Yeshua, who radiated and mirrored to everyone during his time on Earth, but only those with eyes to see and ears to hear could perceive him. Most were blinded by their religious pride and traditions and couldn't accept his teachings. If he were to incarnate now, I am certain the same response would occur because there are conditions necessary to perceive God.

> Blessed are the pure in heart,
> For they shall see God.
>
> ~ Gospel of John 5:8

There are conditions to becoming empty of 'self' and 'ego', and emptying one's cup (with humility) is a significant part of it. Once again, I refer to the story of 'Mary and Martha'. Mary had discovered the key to Yeshua's life. As he sat face-to-face with his Heavenly Father, Mary desired to sit face-to-face with Yeshua, listening, gazing, and watching in stillness and silence as her teacher spoke. Once you uncover this key for yourself, nothing in life will be of more concern to you.

BEING A REFLECTION

For now, we see in a mirror, dimly, but then face to face.

Now I know in part, but then I shall know just as I also am known.

~ 1 Corinthians 13:12

We all understand that a reflection is produced when light bounces off an object. The appearance of the reflection is influenced by the object's texture, whether it is rough or smooth, polished or transparent. A clear reflection can be seen when light rays bounce off a smooth and still surface, such as a pool of water, a still lake, or a mirror.

If we imagine our True Essence as the radiance of the sun, it can be blocked or covered by the ever-changing shapes and density of clouds, which can alter the appearance of the sun. At times, the sun may even seem to have vanished, but the truth is that it hasn't changed in its ability to shine, even if it has been distorted at one level. It is still there in all its beauty, character, and radiance, waiting to burst through the clouds. This is comparable to our true image and likeness, our Buddha nature, Christ nature, or, if you prefer, your True Self. Clouds can alter the atmosphere by blocking light or trapping heat. Some clouds are heavy, while others are light and fluffy, but they all share one characteristic: they all pass, much like our thoughts and emotions do.

Clouds can be seen as a metaphor for thoughts and emotions or even situations that may be causing you to feel heavy, sad, depressed or anxious, thus blocking the Light of your innate Being and preventing it from shining through and into your life. But remember, like all clouds, they will pass, change and move to the next.

Now let's go deeper into how we become the clear reflection of our True Self, that which we already are, our innate Being. In several middle-eastern texts, the **refiner's fire**, and the ***furnace for gold***, are often mentioned (e.g. *Book of Malachi 5:3, Proverbs 17:3, Job 23:10*). Why fire and why gold? Firstly, gold is a precious metal that requires refining to clear its impurities and become pure gold. Intense heat and fire are necessary to remove all the impurities. At the base level, many contaminants attach to gold, such as dirty sand, grit, gravel, and other chemicals. The process of removing the dirt and refining the gold is lengthy and arduous.

The dirt washer must first place the gold in a vat and continue the cleaning process until every bit of dirt, mineral, and chemical has been completely removed. The Goldsmith then places the gold in the crucible and applies intense fire and heat to release all the dross and contaminants. Once the gold is refined and becomes luminous, clear, and radiant, and the Goldsmith can see his reflection, he considers the work of purification complete, and the gold becomes pure gold.

If we apply the analogy of the purification process to our own lives, it can be compared to a soul that turns away from selfishness and toward a life of selflessness, desiring to seek pure things such as love and compassion. However, just as impurities attach themselves to gold, our lives on earth are also filled with patterns that attract impurities. The true definition of impurities, according to the texts, can be anything that dilutes, pollutes, and taints who we are, separating us from our awakened selfless nature and preventing us from knowing the incredible loving presence that is inherent in all of us.

So, we need to take these impurities seriously because they are covering and distorting our very *essence*, deluding us into thinking and believing that an attachment to these impurities is standard when in reality, it is separating us from our True Origins. In the Dhammapada, the sayings of the Buddha, there is a portion on *impurity*:

You are the yellow leaf.

The messengers of death are at hand.

You are to travel far away.

What will you take with you?

You are a lamp

To lighten the way,

Then hurry, hurry.

When your Light shines

Without impurity or desire

You will come into a boundless country.

Your life is falling away.

Death is at hand.

Where will you rest on the way?

What have you taken with you?

You are the lamp

To lighten the way.

Then hurry, hurry.

As a silversmith sifts dust from the silver,

Remove your won impurities

Little by little.

"You are the lamp", the Buddha lovingly reminds us, as Yeshua also proclaimed, *"you are the light of the world"*. So, hurry and live! Hurry and let your light shine! Hurry and stop chasing the material world that is here today and gone tomorrow. Live! Hurry, for you are the lamp; you are light, and let all the impurities fall by the wayside as you sit in the light. The hills melt like wax in the presence of the light. Hurry and let us treat our neighbours well, and by that, I don't just mean humans, but also our trees, our lakes, our forests, our animals, our insects, all that is living and part of life, OUR life. Live, hurry and drop the destructive views we are holding onto. Hurry and remove the ill-wills we cling to, such as unforgiveness, greed, bitterness, and anger, which are slowly corrupting and destroying us. Hurry and drop destructive speech. Quickly drop anything harmful to yourself and harmful to those around you.

You are the lamp, my brother and sister; let your light shine brightly so that all may be encouraged to do likewise.

You are the Light of the world. A city that is set on a hill cannot be hidden.

Nor do they light a lamp and put it under a basket, but on a lampstand,

and it gives Light to all *who are* in the house.

- Gospel of Matthew 5:14-15

TO LOVE THYSELF

I have slowly come to understand what true loving oneself means. It's not about our ability to love ourselves because we have been told to, or because we seek to love ourselves. As it is written, the key is to allow ourselves to love and be loved, and in doing so, we allow Love to overflow in our lives. Love is the very fibre of who we are, and it is the creative force behind the Universe. However, this experience cannot come from reading or simply believing words on a page. Instead, it requires deep reflection, as we soon discover the protective walls we have placed around our hearts that prevent us from experiencing and expressing this divine flow of energy. Only when we dissolve these protective layers and put the "sword" down can we experience our true selves.

"People cannot simply switch a button on to love themselves and others, especially if they have been rejected or raised in an atmosphere where unconditional love is absent. It takes time and trust to love oneself and others. We are creatures that are formed and shaped by experiences and habits. One might be afraid to love in case of rejection, and placing walls of safety seems only natural to them, understandably so when the world can often be a cruel place.

Can you imagine being told that what you are is not good enough and believing it for most of your life? Or what if your parents, for economic reasons, handed you over to someone else to care for, and you were never told but found out only later in life? Do you think loving yourself would come easy? Of course not. How can we expect a soul to suddenly love themselves when they could easily be covered in a garment of self-hatred or thoughts and feelings of self-rejection? The protective walls first have to come tumbling down, and this can only happen if you look deeply into your own heart with an attitude of a loving friend. As though you were holding your heart in your hands and asking, "Am I treating you with loving-kindness? Am I treating you as my very best friend?"

My very close teacher once asked me, *"Steve, how do you treat your heart? Do you treat your sacred centre as though it was your very best friend? Does it have the space to breathe and express itself as it wishes to?"* These questions were the beginnings and early seeds being sown in me that slowly allowed me to look inside myself. Before that, I was a very protective, hurt, and suppressed young man. I remember doing this exercise and seeing a cart-horse: overworked, burdened, and with very little space in its cart. My heart was filled with unwanted memories and crippling emotions that I had tried so hard to forget and suppress, causing pain that led to even more suffering. I did my best not to arouse or think about them, hoping that they would magically vanish with time and never return. But they always did.

One needs to be taught how to deal with pain at school. We are taught an average of nine subjects, yet none is about coping with pain or suffering. As a result, we tend to emulate what we see everyone else doing: running away from it, disguising it, suppressing it, or using stimulants to distract ourselves. But these are only forms of suppressants. Like all forms of energy, pain will continue to linger and transform into more dense energy, which can eventually cause sickness and disease. Only when we learn to open up to Love can we face these energies and ultimately allow them to pass through us. It is a beautiful experience to open up and see trapped feelings as empty images to which we have been attached. It is ultimately our fear of pain that holds us back. When we allow these feelings to dissolve and pass like clouds, one by one, in the non-gripping space of Love, we can return home to our hearts as true, loving friends.

Here is a beautiful story of how Love can take someone at their lowest point, heal them and bring them back home to their True Self. It is the story of a woman caught in the act of adultery. It is the story of Mary of Magdala and how Love stooped down and healed her entirely.

Then the scribes and Pharisees brought to Him a woman caught in adultery. And when they had set her in the midst, they said to Him, "Teacher, this woman was caught in adultery, in the very act. Now Moses, in the law, commanded us that such should be stoned. But what do You say?" This they said, testing Him, that they might have *something* of which to accuse Him. But Jesus stooped down and wrote on the ground with *His* finger as though He did not hear. So when they continued asking Him, He raised Himself up and said to them, "He who is without sin among you, let him throw a stone at her first." And again, He stooped down and wrote on the ground. Then those who heard *it,* being convicted by *their* conscience, went out one by one, beginning with the oldest *even* to the last. And Jesus was left alone, and the woman standing in the midst. When Jesus had raised Himself up and saw no one but the woman,

He said to her, "Woman, where are those accusers of yours?

Has no one condemned you?" She said, "No one, Lord."

And Jesus said to her, "Neither do I condemn you; go and sin no more."

Then Jesus spoke to them again, saying, "I am the light of the world.

He who follows Me shall not walk in darkness, but have the light of life."

- Gospel of John 8:3-12

Love is always listening to the voice of loving-kindness, wisdom, and truth. Love sees the journey of a soul, its choices, and the law of causation all at once. Love always stoops down, reaches out with wisdom and understanding, and brings healing in its wings. Love often waits for us and remains silent until we are ready to listen. Love doesn't impose itself, yet it is always here. Yeshua was writing a new law on the Earth when he stooped down. Man had the Ten Commandments that Moses gave, written on stone tablets. Yeshua wrote on the living Earth as if writing on the tablets of our hearts, 'the Law of *Love'*. He, too, could have condemned the men with their law, but He didn't. So here was wisdom speaking, touching not only the heart of Mary with unconditional love and forgiveness, but His words also touched the core and essence of those men convicted by their conscience.

Yeshua demonstrated that deep listening to our Sacred Centre brings healing, forgiveness, and release. But first, we must stoop down to our hearts, connect, commune, and look through Love's lens. We should speak and act upon that, rather than react to the noise from the outside. That moment of Mary's encounter with the mirror of Love caused her to return to her True Self—the one she had lost for so many years and had been seeking. The Self she had lost through pain, rejection, and abuse, the one she thought she would never be able to find again. It was the first time in her life that she felt a new surge of hope run through her veins. The face-to-face and heart-to-heart encounter empowered her to walk in a completely different direction from where she was going.

BROKEN HEARTS

Most people worldwide have experienced a broken heart at some point in their lives. For some, it happens early on through losing a loved one or experiencing a break-up in a relationship. For others, it may happen later in life. But one thing is for sure, wherever you go around the world, you will find that people have this in common. There can be multiple reasons for a broken heart, often due to a loss, break-up in a relationship, or not getting what you wanted or expected after investing time and energy into a relationship. There is a common thread of giving one's heart, emotions, time, and energy, only to have that relationship break, leaving a sense of pain, loss, and sometimes, emptiness. Perhaps you didn't receive help or support growing up, studied and worked hard, but forgot to check in with your heart, this sacred part of you that influences every aspect of your life.

The media also paint many misconceptions about relationships. So most people growing up end up mirroring other people's relationships, those closest to them, usually their parents or other family members.

If you observe the people closest to you who pretend that everything is fine, suppress and deny painful emotions, and say things like 'just get on with it!' this is likely the habit you will adopt for yourself when you have a similar experience. We cannot blame people for rebelling or going off the rails; they often suffer from depression or anxiety and don't have the energy or willpower to make a change. With the current pace of the material world, people are driving themselves to meet the constant demand for more. The rise of the internet and social media platforms is causing even greater distractions, leaving people with little time to stop, inquire within, and listen to the gentle whispers of their hearts.

One of the Four Noble Truths that the Buddha taught is **dukkha** in Sanskrit, meaning *suffering*. The Buddha taught that in life, one would suffer, feeling the strain of getting old in our bodies, suffer because others suffer, or suffer when life doesn't happen as we would like. He also taught about the ***causation of suffering***. Why do we suffer, and *how* do we suffer when we crave and attach ourselves to objects, beliefs or ideas in an ever-changing impermanent world and gripping with a notion of an "I", "me", and "myself" that is separate and independent. Then you live that egoic life by holding on to it dearly. The good news is that he also taught a ***path that leads to the end of suffering***.

So, let's explore this wisdom and see if it touches some chords in your heart. Have you ever asked yourself why your emotions initially caused us so much pain? Most people believe their heart needs to be given in a relationship; if it's not, it's not good enough. On one level, you need to give your time, commitment, devotion and dedication, but how can one give their heart *away*?

If we observe an open flower, we can see the beauty of all the colours it shares with us, the sweet-smelling fragrance, and how pleasant it is for the eyes to behold, blessing us with its beauty and fragrance. It is not meant to be given but shared. We can share our songs, words, poetry, affection, and love with all. But if we give our hearts away, they lose their alignment, and once they lose their alignment, they lose their peace. Our hearts are not meant to be given because they carry our imprints, inner convictions, individual and authentic sounds, and expressions. These aspects of our lives are our light, fragrance, and gift to all humanity. So please, my brothers and sisters, don't give your precious heart away, fixing it to any idea, belief, or person because everything in life moves on and changes.

Everything is subject to these laws, so travel and walk lightly. Love all sentient beings and share your warm smile. And if you have been hurt because you gave your heart away and said, "I am never going into another relationship again," please don't be afraid. From now on, you can open your heart again. Only, don't give it away. Share it with those who will respect you and walk with you. Smile and move on from those who won't, but don't be afraid to enter another relationship. And if you are suffering from a broken heart, feel these words. Your heart is meant to be shared, but not with everyone. Your heart needs to open to feel life and experience it wholeheartedly, like the sunflower that opens and receives the light of the sun.

If you have agreed with your heart to protect and close it, I fully understand. But my dear friend, you are only delaying its healing. We all suffer, but we suffer much more when we grip and hold on, trying to control, subdue, and forget the pain. On the other hand, if you open your heart again and allow yourself to share again, the energy will move and pass through. Soon your inner smile will return. Only this time, you will know the secret of never giving your heart away, only sharing its fragrance, accepting that some will enjoy it and others may not. There's nothing to fear. We all have to face and walk through suffering in our lives.

> Blessed *are* the pure in heart,
> For they shall see God.
> － Gospel of Matthew 5:8

A pure heart open to the light,

will be filled with the essence of Truth

-   Rumi

When Rumi said a ***"heart open to the light"***, he meant the same as Yeshua when he said, ***"those who have a pure heart shall see God"***, for our hearts carry a fragrance of light, and this light was there from the beginning of Eternity. It is our very nature and our true essence, our power. But to access this light, we must learn to keep it open, sharing the fragrance of loving-kindness with all and not grasping on to the view that this is your life, but **ours**.

MELTING THE EGO

When talking about one's ego self, I am referring to that part of the self that feels and thinks it is separated from the All, as though it is living as an individual and separate existence from everything and everyone else. This happens when we lose our awareness of the Presence given to us at birth. We were all blessed with an unstained and unmoved Presence called Awareness. This Awareness is outside the domain of attachment and clinging, as it is free from all forms of suffering. It is often called our True Self, Christ in You, Buddha Mind, or Pure Mind. It has always been there and will always remain there.

The question is, where is there? It's always been here. Where is here? It's now, ever present, rooted without a root because it needs nothing, it exists as existence itself, and this is the actual abiding state described as *Awareness happening by itself.*

So, where does the ego exist, then? The moment we adopt an idea or construct that suggests we exist outside of this moment, we soon develop the experience of a small 'self' or 'me' that feels separate from Awareness. This separation causes us to become self-concerned and self-conscious, which causes us to lose the ability to feel the beautiful, peaceful Presence that we all possess. As a result, we create feelings of wrongdoing, guilt, shame, and other forms of negative emotions because we don't feel like we match what the world is projecting onto us. This leads to further experiences of agitation, anxiety, depression, and nervousness. This is why self-help, when done outside of Awareness, doesn't work. It only creates more noise and conflicting ideas.

However, the ego self, with time, can lose its grip on your life, and you can return wholeheartedly to your beautiful bright Awareness, living in this world mindfully and peacefully without suffering. Sounds impressive. It's honestly true, and this is what the Buddha was teaching when he taught the Four Noble Truths, otherwise interpreted as 'Truths to the Noble Ones':

Dukkha - *the Truth of Suffering*
Samudaya - *the Cause of Suffering*
Nirodha - *the End of Suffering*
Magga - *the Path that leads out of Suffering*

We suffer when we live in the dimension and idea that we are a separate self - we grip like mad, trying to hold on to this life but soon discover that whatever we grab onto changes because all things are impermanent and subject to the Law of Impermanence.

Whosoever wants to save their life will lose it,

but whoever loses their life will find it.

—   *Gospel of Matthew 16:25*

We can only lose what we cling to. So, when we first lose our awareness, our instinct is to cling on because we feel we are losing something precious. But the truth is, that which is and always was cannot be lost. It's there waiting patiently and lovingly, always ready to shine through us and for us. It's a force, an inner light that is the result waiting to be discovered. A perfectly finished result that is complete in its original state and needs no effort or extra work to give it more shine, beauty, or brightness. It's the beginning and the end, all in one.

The ego 'self' separates us from knowing this. It forms a life of chasing, grabbing, pushing, and searching for this presence, creating a life outside of truth and spinning a web of karma - traces of energy that often have a life of their own, turning into thoughts and constructs that are delusional. But recognizing that we are not these thoughts, ideas, and constructs by becoming aware is the beginning stage in dissolving the ego-self. Giving ourselves the space to watch these thoughts and not feeding them will slowly but surely stop the wheels from spinning further and further away into these false delusional patterns. True presence is then allowed to manifest through the heart, mind, and feelings. Once you arrive at this place, allowing yourself to yield to your inner light and offering zero resistance, living in presence becomes your everyday abiding existence. The joy of your abiding, peaceful presence will always be there for you to enjoy the beauty of this life once again, as you did when you were light, free, and happy as a child.

YOU ARE STILLNESS

Nowadays, if I were to say to people, *"you are stillness"*, most would say I was crazy, delusional and deceived but most people today are overworked, overstimulated, overthinking, have too much on their minds, and are filled with worries and concerns about their economics and consumed with making a living or just trying to make ends meet. In a way, they would be correct because the vast majority of people are so far away from their calm-abiding ever-present stillness. Most people are in a state where they are spinning stories and getting wrapped up in them, their minds jumping from one drama to the next, unable to be present. And most would call this a 'normal' existence, feeling easily distracted or bored because we have slowly become a generation of fast food and overstimulated thoughts, moving from one thing to the next. But beneath all that stimulation, distraction, and noise is a stillness that is fully present and aware of this moment. Just because your thoughts are jumping, it doesn't mean your awareness is not in stillness. The stillness behind every sensation and thought is you, the true essence of your mind. I refer to this stillness as your natural, authentic primordial space that's always quietly abiding there, waiting patiently and lovingly for your mind to return to it. You experience it in moments of art, music, sports, or when you are engaged in an intimate conversation with a friend and not self-conscious. The moment and your awareness become one, and the concept of time and separation suddenly evaporate. Yet we call this having a joyful time and often say how quickly time passes. To further explain that you are stillness at the quintessence, let me share a famous story of a traveling monk who was captivated by a free bird flying over the Himalayan peaks.

These intimate and beautiful moments took place on a mountain where a Monk had been sitting quietly for weeks, enjoying the peace and breath-taking scenery. His favourite pastime was to find the peak of the mountain and stay there with the birds of prey that often gathered there. One day, the birds noticed the new-looking stranger with his warm woolly hat and brightly coloured gowns, but their distrust of humans kept them constantly at a distance and watching with deep caution. As time went by, the Monk continued his daily practice of merging with the stillness of the mountain and sinking into a beautiful surrendered stillness, forming a union with peace itself as if only stillness itself was the experience. As a result, the birds stopped noticing the Monk and soon perched on his motionless body, using him like a tree branch. The mountain, the Monk, and the birds had become one, as if they were all an extension of the same peace, harmonizing in the Presence and joining forces with the nearby lakes, trees, and clouds until motion and stillness were one. He often used this as a sign that his meditation practice was working, and when he journeyed to the nearby villages, he would often do the same with nervous strangers. Peace, compassion, and joy are all birthed from stillness when we let go and drop both mind and body, allowing these beautiful expressions of energy to be transmitted and experienced by all living creatures. Every human knows this is true because we have all felt the opposite manifestations of energy, like anger or hatred, and have seen their effect on all our lives. I can still remember the first time my father became extremely angry with me and shouted, or the time my PE teacher threw me down some school steps because I wouldn't play for his rugby team. These powerful transfers of energy can lead to tremendous suffering, especially when you are a child in development, or on the other hand, if the energies are transmitted with loving compassion, it can lead to a beautiful and transformative experience.

Exchanges await us every day, and we can all choose to be an instrument for peace, joy, and compassion. By radiating these qualities from our beings, we can bring kindness to everyone we come into contact with, if we allow ourselves to drop our defenses and merge with stillness. However, before we can become useful instruments, we must first realize that we are stillness waiting to appear in every area of our lives. Therefore, we must give stillness an opportunity and make room for it in our lives, as it is the very nature of our presence and the language of our Source.

This intimate expression and experience of life is why we live here on earth - to live and enjoy every moment in its fullness without being conscious of what others may think or say. Just like the monk who was able to impact the birds to forget their caution, we can also influence others to live wholeheartedly. We can live in this beauty and intimacy if we let go without resistance to the call of stillness, as though we were children falling into our parents' loving and trusted arms.

We can trust Stillness wholeheartedly as we know that it offers spaciousness, is non-judgmental, pure, calm-abiding, and reveals truth moment by moment. It is complete awareness - a real trusted guide and gentle friend that leads our lives and navigates us through all our suffering. In this stillness, we find our inner ears open and our internal eyes awakened as though a veil had been removed, and now the path ahead is clear. Stillness has become the ocean we swim in, and the currents that move us are silence. This majestic stillness and silence are the roots of everything that exists. It is the place we all sprung forth from, the space all life is birthed from, and all will one day return to.

STOP!

I want to delve deeper into the story of Aṅgulimāla, the bloodthirsty terrorist who lived during the time of the Buddha, with you. He was a man who dedicated his entire life to killing and terrorizing others, and even wore a garland around his neck made from the fingers of his victims. However, his encounter with the Buddha changed the course of his life entirely:

One day, the Buddha was staying in the area where Aṅgulimāla lived. While he was out doing his daily alms, he decided to visit Aṅgulimāla with the intention of reaching his true heart and nature. The local farmers and residents warned the Buddha that it was not a safe place for him and urged him to turn back. However, the Buddha continued walking with a clear heart and mind, radiating peace and loving-kindness with every step. He moved closer to where Aṅgulimāla was settled.

When Aṅgulimāla saw the lone Monk pass by, he saw an opportunity to kill him and ran towards him. However, no matter how slow the Buddha walked or how fast Aṅgulimāla ran towards him, he could never reach him to strike him with his sword. Eventually, Aṅgulimāla got tired of chasing and cried out, "Stop! Stop!! I command you to stop!!!" The Buddha replied, "I have stopped Aṅgulimāla. You are the one that needs to stop."

Aṅgulimāla was extremely tired and perplexed, so he asked the Buddha, "You say you have stopped, but you are walking, and I have stopped, and you say I need to stop. What is the meaning of this?" The Buddha replied, "I have stopped, once and for all. I have cast off all violence towards all sentient beings. You, however, are unrestrained towards beings. That's how I have stopped, and you are still going."

Moved by the words of the Buddha, Aṅgulimāla immediately turned from his wicked ways, hurled his weapons off a nearby cliff, and requested to become a student without any delay. This story can be interpreted in many different and beautiful ways. It may call upon us to abandon all our wicked ways or to realize the power we all have to make an immediate change in our lives, no matter how far we have lost ourselves. Alternatively, from the Buddha's perspective, the story may inspire us to reach out to all sentient beings, even when the crowds tell us to stay away out of fear. The story also highlights the level of trust that the Buddha had in the Sacred Spirit to know that Aṅgulimāla was even reachable.

In *Romans 8:14* of the New Testament, a text expresses it this way: *"For all who are led by the spirit of God are sons of God."*

There are so many beautiful keys and parts to this story, but I want to focus on the **stop** that Angulimala experienced. The shock of chasing someone you are determined to kill and yet, never being able to reach this slow walking and peaceful soul. I want you to feel the anger, the violent thoughts and madness of one lost soul who has developed an unquenchable desire to capture this liberated soul, grasping at an empty loving spirit-soul being who has ascended and has become translucent, spacious, free and floating along with the entire Cosmos.

In the case of Aṅgulimāla, the **flesh** and the density of heavily burdened matter are chasing the **spirit**. The two are in conflict; one is weighed down by the attachments and lower vibrations of the lost nature, while the other is free, light and one with all that is.

Flesh gives birth to flesh, but the spirit gives birth to spirit.

- Gospel of John 3:6

A person may live on this earth and create a life that generates dense and heavy negative karma, causing suffering for oneself and others. In contrast, another person may carry light and love wherever they go, creating peace and well-being for those they encounter. No matter how fast Aṅgulimāla chased after the Buddha, he could not catch him because the soul weighed down by attachment to material things is like a huge burden on its shoulders, causing suffering until it becomes tired and stops chasing. Many teachers have delivered the same message to humanity.

The message of STOP! Is a profound and prophetic message by one of the greatest teachers that graced our earth? Buddha was calling Aṅgulimāla to stop, but I hear his voice calling out to all of us, whispering, "*Stop, my dear brother and sister, while you have the chance. Stop the wheels from spinning and return home immediately while you still have a chance. Stop and drop everything, and you will experience the sweet nature of the most wonderful indwelling peace. So, stop, my beloved brother and sister, for we are one, and there is an end to this suffering. There is a path that leads to the end of all suffering, for you have spun in the wrong direction, but now you can stop the wheels and come home. Come home and find shelter, a resting place, and an eternal refuge for your soul.*"

CONTEMPLATION & REFLECTION

Please find a warm and comfortable place to sit with your spine nice and straight. Allow your heart to be filled with immense gratitude, as if it were being filled with the warm and loving rays of the sun, or the best and most sacred memories you have of a loving friend or loved one. Become aware of your sacred breath, inhaling and exhaling. Can you feel the ocean and the waves in your in and out breath?

Notice that it's breathing you effortlessly. Life is living through you and for you, and no effort is required as you contemplate this poem. It was written from my heart to yours with immense love and a deep sense of how sacred your life is. I truly see you, even if you may not know it or sense it. Your life is beautiful, and so are you. I hope that when you read these words, some part of you will begin to feel the love that you truly are.

YOU ARE LOVED

Every part of you is loved,
This is why your real name is *beloved*,
Your soul wrapped in a glove,
From the Eternal Light above.

When you sit and rise
You have always been the prize.
A treasure,
Always my great pleasure.
Chosen like the ocean
You have been woven,
With waves of love.

You are truly loved, my beloved,

With devotion,

A wild explosion,

You came into motion.

The flowers bloom,

The same way you came out of your mother's womb.

The stars shine,

They sparkle and wink,

Every time you think.

You are so loved,

Without you, this entire universe

Wouldn't be the same,

It's your name that's a light-loving flame.

Only you have forgotten how loved you are.

Your life, your name, this burning flame,

It was all birthed when you came.

You're a treasured piece of the whole,

The wave and the ocean,

The star and the space,

The Sun and the moon,

A beautifully constructed tune.

You say "dust to dust"

But I say, "from glory to glory."

You say, "I am just an accident."
I say, "perfectly woven, my beloved, chosen."
An everlasting spirit,
Created by a song of love,
Loved from Eternity,
With a steadfast certainty.
I knew your name before you were born,
Before the foundations of the Earth,
I was totally aware of your worth.
And I always wait for our loving date.
In this, there is no debate.

You are loved,
Treasured,
Never judged or measured.
My love is unconditional,
Because it's the fountain of the Original.
You are loved,
Until the last breath,
What you call death.

CHAPTER 3

SUFFERING AND PAIN

Before we delve into the subject of suffering and pain, it's important to make a clear distinction between the two as they are closely related. **Pain** refers to what is happening to us, the natural physical sensation we feel in the moment. **Suffering**, on the other hand, is how we deal with the pain, manage it, and what we do with the energy of hurt when it arises. At some point in our lives, we will all experience pain, which may manifest as physical or emotional pain - both very different experiences but equally important. However, what's surprising is that nowhere in our academic institutions is the subject of pain management ever discussed or examined. Our entire society seems to be trying its best to avoid it, yet pain is probably one of the most important factors in our lives and the force that shapes our personalities the most.

In the previous chapter, I mentioned the life of Aṅgulimāla, but I didn't mention the emotional pain he would have felt watching his parents being mistreated because they were considered of a lower caste. This pain led to his agreement to be respected at all costs. However, pain begets pain and further suffering if we don't know how to manage it wisely.

What purpose and gain can pain have in our lives then? When we experience physical pain, such as a pulled muscle or joint pain, it serves as a clear signal that we need to rest, slow down, warm up better, drink more water, or stretch. Sometimes, achy joints can indicate excessive weight or nutritional deficiencies. These are all signs that we need to take action. It is nature's way of communicating with us. Therefore, pain can be seen as a friend that warns us of something in our lives that requires attention. The same is true for emotional distress, rejection, being laughed at, or losing someone we love. These genuine sensations, including a heavy heart, stress, tightness, and anxiety leading to mild panic attacks, are experienced by many people daily. However, few know how to manage and cope with these energies. Often, people tend to focus on negative thoughts rather than examining the potential causes of their feelings and why they are focusing on the adverse effects of their experiences. They may also question why life did not happen the way they wanted it to. However, I want you to know with all my heart and love that I am not blaming or judging anyone or any situation they may be facing.

As I mentioned, these things are not taught, so one automatically imitates those in front of and around them. Unfortunately, most people are doing the same thing with pain: running away from it, denying it's there, masking it, or suppressing it until it turns into an agreement of revenge like Aṅgulimāla, or with frequent outbursts of anger. Unless this is openly taught in our society, our academic institutions, and at every level of a child's development into adulthood, the wheels of suffering, reactions, and prolonged pain will continue to spiral from one generation to the next. The same mess will continue to transfer, but with more distractions and artificial ways of dealing with it. If we continue to avoid the message and purpose of these feelings, the pain will only transform and create further suffering.

As human beings, we will face difficult situations at every stage of our development. There is no denying this. We all know rejection hurts, especially when it's the first time we experience it, and especially when it's from someone we love or respect. The result of grief, regret, loss, shame, and failure can all lead to feelings of loneliness, anger, depression, and even actions of desperation. Despite our technological advances and improvements, suicide, anxiety, and depression have all increased.

Now you can understand why the Buddha wanted to tackle and face pain and suffering, experience it, and find a way to the end of it. He warned us that life is suffering, not because it is, but because he wanted us to accept it and meet it face-on, as he did. By doing so, we can see it, accept it as a part of our lives, and not run away or mismanage it. Suppressing strong emotions like a broken heart will only delay the energy from moving and passing on. A close friend once told me that when a bad relationship broke his precious heart, he agreed to close his heart, afraid of it happening again. It took him a total of fourteen years to fully recover. You must understand that these energies will change; eventually, the Law of Impermanence is a law we can trust. Everything changes eventually, so holding on, wanting revenge, not forgiving, and holding on to things that harm us only cause us more pain. Yet if we allow these energies to surface as they are, giving them space to move, they will, and it won't take long.

My dear friend, if we observe nature, we can see that everything is constantly changing, passing from one form to the next, from one season to the next, non-grasping, and flowing with the moment. This is the power of true, beautiful acceptance. It deals with the moment of reality as it is, allowing it the space to be what it is, and eventually, like everything in life, it will move and change. Letting go is a powerful act of liberation, and it's a choice we can all make, fully appreciating all that is in this moment and facing things head-on, wholeheartedly, without any fear. For it is fear that holds on, it is fear that grasps and doesn't want to change. But true power is allowing things to be what they are, real power, absolute love, and the way to see pain as a friend who speaks when there needs to be a beautiful change that we never need to fear again. How freeing is that?

There is no fear in love. Perfect love casts out all fear.

- 1 John 4:18

If you realise that all things change, there is nothing you will try to hold on to.

If you are not afraid of dying, there is nothing you cannot achieve.

- Lao Tzu (Tao Te Ching)

Blessed are those who mourn, for they shall be comforted.

- Gospel of Matthew 5:4

The lowly he sets on high, and those who mourn are lifted into safety.

- Job 5:11

To everything, there is a season and a time to every purpose under the heaven:

A time to be born and a time to die, a time to plant,

and a time to pluck up that which is planted;

A time to kill, and a time to heal; a time to break down,

and a time to build up;

A time to weep, and a time to laugh;

a time to mourn, and a time to dance;

A time to cast away stones, and a time to gather stones together;

a time to embrace and a time to refrain from embracing;

A time to get and a time to lose; a time to keep, and a time to cast away;

A time to rend, and a time to sew; a time to keep silence, and a time to speak;

A time to love and a time to hate, a time of war, and a time of peace.

- Book of Ecclesiastes 3:1-8

SACRED 24

One of the most beautiful things we all experience and share in our lives is the sacred 24-hour **cycle**. At times, we take this cycle for granted and live our days as though they are everyday routines, adopting the view that today or tomorrow is just another ordinary day with the same old stuff as the previous day. But upon closer examination, we find that this couldn't be further from the truth. Every moment in our lives is unique, authentic, and different if we allow it to pass without clinging to the past.

Think about the constantly moving clouds, creating new shapes and patterns, or the birds moving from one place to the next, or the trees dropping their leaves with squirrels moving up and around, suddenly spotted by a dog whose hair rises and springs out, running, trying to climb the tree to no avail. At the same time, someone passes you on a bike, listening to their headphones, and suddenly the light changes as the clouds cover the sun, and everything looks different. What about the snail moving beneath your feet, the ants working in unison ten meters away, or the coffee being made twenty meters away in a coffee shop for someone running late? All of this happens in just a few minutes, but we might miss it because we're too worried about yesterday or what could be coming.

Every moment in our lives is full of newness, magic, wonder, and change. Motion, movement, and action occur all the time in every place, everywhere, and we call this life. One 24-hour cycle has everything we need if we are open to accepting it as a teacher.

We know that we need resistance to grow and be challenged at times to improve. We also need experience to develop and mature in our confidence. We don't suddenly grow up knowing everything and being good at everything. Learning takes time and consistency before we can master it. As children, we were happy to learn new things every day at our own pace. We learned how to string a sentence, ride a bike, skate, read a book, throw stones, draw a house, or climb everything and everywhere. Our development was different for everyone, as some kids developed quicker in art or math, others in science and literature, and some excelled in sports. It was a unique and sacred individual experience for everyone.

When we allowed ourselves to learn naturally without pressure or expectations, it was fun and beautiful. Making mistakes and tripping over were all part of it. We would laugh and keep going. However, as we grew older, we became more serious and fearful. We were afraid to sing, ask someone out, make friends, or dance. We became paralyzed by the fear of being laughed at or rejected. The small 'self' placed expectations on our true self, quenching the very life out of us. Our 24-hour cycle became controlled by a box of fear, limiting us and stealing the extraordinary potential of life and learning opportunities.

Living in this tight box of fear will only keep us there. One 24-hour cycle feeds the next, creating negative cycles and stealing the joy of life. Eventually, we may become tired, fed up, miserable, or even depressed. By then, we may be too frail or sick to recover. Instead, we need to let go and allow life to be life. We may trip over, make mistakes, fail, get laughed at, or rejected, but who cares? We need to live in the moment and embrace life's experiences. Only then can we learn, grow, and develop into the best version of ourselves.

This is why every 24 hours offer you a magical opportunity to make changes, to stop old patterns of fear from spinning, and start creating new wheels of letting life be what it is without caring so much about the outcome but rather living the experience. Nothing is lacking in your 24-hour cycle. Everything you need to journey further in your life is there, waiting to reveal itself if you allow it and if you return to being that childlike soul that wants to discover and live without any expectations. The whole world belongs to you if you live this way; every macro and micro experience is yours when you live like this because you merge with the moment, the Eternal Moment, and all that is living in that moment - it all belongs to you.

How wonderful and magical is that? Of course, this will take courage, and you will feel nervous and challenged. You will probably invent excuses for why you can't, why you shouldn't, and why you won't. But it will only happen if you make some effort. Action is necessary! It requires movement and motion in directions that make you uncomfortable and even painful. It's not going to happen just by wishing for it, trying to feel the experience, and then hoping that, by some mystical way without action, it will turn up at your doorstep under the Law of Attraction. Thinking about it may be helpful when you are lying in bed creating some fantasies, feeling it may give you a moment of inspiration and even cause the hair on your body to rise, but it will not turn the wheels. The truth reveals the way; you must walk the way to experience life. Three is the magic number. The **truth**, the **way**, and the **life** work together wonderfully. But are you prepared to walk the way once the truth has revealed the light in your situation?

So, what are you waiting for? Every magical moment is a sparkling new opportunity for you to embrace your 24-hour cycle with wholeheartedness and give your heart and mind the adventure they crave, like the experiences you once lived as a child, full of wonder, joy, and laughter. We still don't know how much time we have left. We can't decide how many more 24-hour cycles we will get. Time is fleeting, always moving, and waits for no one. Since you can't control it, why not live it fully and venture into your new beginning?

The end is another beginning.

  - Rumi

Let go or be dragged.

  - Zen Proverb

Nothing ever goes away until it has taught us what we need to know.

  - Chodron

LESSONS OF LOVE

We all face challenging times in our lives. Sometimes, it may seem as though a shadow is constantly following us, causing us to suffer and hurt ourselves and others. However, one day we may come to realize that the shadow was never real, as it could not exist without light. The shadow was merely a delusion brought about by a state of ignorance. This is similar to when we prevent ourselves from shining, either because we are afraid to be our true selves, or because we feel a large shadow covering our minds, causing us to contract and shrink until we feel like mere shadows of our true selves.

I would like to remind you to move beyond any shadows or blockages you may be experiencing and tap into the power of your inner light, which I have come to realize is the same substance that holds the entire universe together - Love. Love is our very essence, our nature, and the force that keeps us alive. Love has formed every fibre of the trillion cells that make up our bodies and allows the majestic creative force within us to thrive. However, we often lose sight of this great force and accept things about ourselves that are not true and damaging. When examining broken families, relationships, or communities, psychologists will tell you that the absence of Love can cause significant damage.

Throughout my fifty years on this planet, I have witnessed how the power of Love can heal broken marriages, lead people into deep forgiveness, and restore broken relationships entirely. Love is a potent force that, when realized and activated correctly, can transform our lives. Yeshua reminded us that Love was the most important of all commandments, laws, and principles to follow. He compared his blood that nourishes the heart to the importance of Love sustaining spiritual life. However, we must be careful about the type of Love we embrace, as there are many expressions of Love, such as romantic love or the love that clings or is fearful of trusting and letting go. This was not the Love that Jesus or Buddha spoke of. The Love they spoke of and demonstrated is a powerful force that can lead souls into absolute freedom, real joy, and liberty if they learn how to trust it, activate it, and allow it to grow and blossom.

Loving-kindness, compassion, joy, and patience do not envy, boast, or point fingers. They are not proud but rather soft and humble, always ready to forgive. Love is not easily angered and keeps no record of wrongdoing. It delights in goodness and is overjoyed when the truth is revealed. These are the qualities, or fruits, of love that we are encouraged to cultivate by these great teachers.

Love is not a wishy-washy or flimsy feeling that arises from watching a romantic episode on Netflix, nor is it an emotional response to a specific day on the calendar or feeling free when things are going well. The love taught and demonstrated by these teachers is the foundation and root of their teachings, and it should not be diluted or polluted into some soft and gooey texture that only appears when the atmosphere is conducive to it.

To love in "good" conditions is not the love that Yeshua taught us to live by. It requires deep meditation, prayer, or long retreats to cultivate this kind of love, and it should not evaporate when we encounter difficult situations or people who are not like-minded or who come from war-torn countries or abusive backgrounds. Loving those who love you is easy, but applying what Yeshua says requires us to love even those who do not love us

Therefore, it is a far greater challenge to commit to loving all beings, especially those who are different from us or have had different life experiences. However, this is the love that Yeshua taught us to embody, and we should strive to cultivate it every day.

"But I say to you who hear: Love your enemies, do good to those who hate you, bless those who curse you, and pray for those who spitefully use you. To him who strikes you on the *one* cheek, offer the other also. And from him who takes away your cloak, do not withhold *your* tunic either. Give to everyone who asks of you. And from him who takes away your goods, do not ask *them* back. And just as you want men to do to you, you also do to them likewise."

- Gospel of Luke 6:27-31

He goes on to say:

"But if you love those who love you, what credit is that to you? For even sinners love those who love them. And if you do good to those who do good to you, what credit is that to you? For even sinners do the same. And if you lend *to those* from whom you hope to receive back, what credit is that to you? For even sinners lend to sinners to receive as much back. But love your enemies, do good, and lend, hoping for nothing in return; and your reward will be great, and you will be sons of the Most High.

For He is kind to the unthankful and evil. Therefore, be merciful, just as your

Father also is merciful."

- Gospel of Luke 32:36

As human beings living in a world where the *"me, myself and I"* rule, the teachings of Yeshua push those boundaries. But to be able to accept his teachings and act upon them, it is essential to truly understand the heart and mind of our Father God, the Creator and the sustenance of our lives.

The Lord has appeared of old to me, *saying:*

"Yes, I have loved you with an everlasting love;

Therefore with lovingkindness, I have drawn you."

- Jeremiah 31:3

No one can know or love someone or something it cannot feel or see. Yet if we look at Yeshua's prayer and communion with his Heavenly Father, we see how very intimate they are through his communication:

"My Righteous Father, although the world has not known you, I have.

I have known you, and these have known that you have sent me.

And I have revealed to them your Name, and I am revealing it so that

the Love with which you have loved me shall be in them, and I shall be

in them." (Yeshua speaking to his Heavenly Father)

- Gospel of John 17:25-26

Yeshua is saying that the love he knows, he knew from before, and was revealing it to his students so that they too could get to know this love. This is why we have needed prophets, teachers, enlightened souls, records, and books to remind us of who we are, where we came from, how loved we are, how precious our life is, and that life can be a most beautiful experience. This is why the first commandment points us to the heavens and the second to love all our neighbours, all living creatures here on earth, and in doing so, we fulfill every other law and commandment. The text reveals that God is love, and we were created from this source, so our essence is love. But to know this love, to experience it, we first need to activate it. It's like opening an eternal wellspring of water once activated. And the following text speaks to all of us who haven't seen God but trust in the words of Yeshua because we have seen the evidence of love work. As I mentioned, it's one of the ways of activating this force in our lives.

"If someone says, 'I love God,' and hates his brother, he is a liar;

for he who does not love his brother whom he has seen, how

can he love God whom he has not seen? And this commandment

we have from Him: that he who loves God *must* love his brother also."

\-   1 John 4:20-21

The way to love the God that we don't see is to love our neighbour who we can see. And who is our neighbour? It is every living creature we come across in every precious 24-hour cycle - all that is living, all that God created. We are to love every living creature - plant, fish, reptile, human, and even those who hate us. This is how God's love is activated and realized. The presence of God is experienced, and His passion is felt in all our beings, allowed to shine through. For God is one, His light is in all of us, and His signature is in all His creation. If we loved our trees, we wouldn't destroy 15 billion of them yearly; they, too, are our neighbours; they also have a purpose and an impact with a role to play. We should consider what love would do instead, as love would lead us to better and brighter ways. Would love abuse animals when around 115 million animals are killed in laboratory experiments worldwide for material gain? Would love allow animals to suffer this way? Would love start wars? Would love rape, murder, or abuse any living beings? No, of course not! Love is kind and compassionate always. The message Yeshua and the Buddha came to reveal and remind us is to return to our **first love**.

BECOMING A SERVANT

One of the most beautiful texts I have ever read is the account of Yeshua stooping down to wash his students' feet in the Gospel of John 13:1-17. This event took place during the last supper that Yeshua would have with his students. It was his final night with them before he would undergo a cruel punishment and torture by man: being beaten, whipped, mocked, spat upon, humiliated, and then nailed to a cross to die - the most horrific torture for those condemned to die. Yeshua had spoken and predicted his death on many occasions, but his students didn't fully understand until it came to pass.

> "The Son of Man will be delivered over to the chief priests and scribes,
> and they will condemn him to death and deliver him over to the Gentiles to be
> mocked and flogged and crucified, and he will be raised on the third day"
>
> ~ Matthew 20:17-19

> Yehsua, knowing that the Father had given all things into His hands,
> and that He had come from God and was going to God, rose from
> supper and laid aside His garments, took a towel and girded Himself.
> After that, He poured water into a basin and began to wash the
> disciples' feet and wipe *them* with the towel with which He was girded.
>
> ~ John 13:3-6

Through this act of service, Yeshua demonstrated to his disciples how much he loved them. He was showing them symbolically how far he was willing to go by laying his life down for them. Despite being a great teacher filled with power and authority, he always put service first and demonstrated this until the very end of his life and ministry.

"Yet it shall not be so among you; but whoever desires to become great among you shall be your servant. And whoever of you desires to be first shall be slave of all. For even the Son of Man did not come to be served, but to serve, and to give His life a ransom for many."

~ Mark 10:43-45

When we take up the call to help all sentient beings and love all of God's creation, and wash each other's feet, we are choosing the path of selflessness, humility, servitude, and unconditional love for all. To clean our neighbour's feet is to stoop down and touch the part of a brother or sister's body that has touched the earth, journeyed with immense pain and suffering, scars of rejection, fears of poverty or neglect, and sometimes wounds from war-torn countries who have lost loved ones. Stopping down with love and humility, washing away all their cares, tension, accumulated stress, and troubles with the love that overflows from the hearts and hands of those who know how deeply loved they are, imparting this love with every stroke, touch, and sweet embrace, leaves them with traces that they may have never felt before. This act is also profoundly symbolic of how we should see others, as it takes us straight to humanity's level. We are here to walk on the sacred earth as equals.

Often, when I sit in deep stillness or prayer, I feel as though the water of the Sacred Presence is washing me with waves and vibrations of currents of unconditional love. A wave of peace breaks open my heart while tears of immense gratitude stream down my face. Then, as though a blanket is placed over me, I am assured that everything will be okay. We are called to love and serve each other like this. When we do, a beautiful highway appears for all to see, an atmosphere of service shines through humility, and where there is humility, forgiveness and reconciliation are always present.

To be a servant is to lead by example, not by words, but by actions that want to lift, encourage and help souls along the path without expecting anything in return. We are called to be givers first, and then it will be returned. For with the measure we give, it will return to us. But it is always better to give than to receive. This is the highest act of love and service.

If you are waiting for something to happen in your life, take this wonderful lesson from washing one's feet and give as though you would want to receive love with the love you want to be loved. But we first must step down, stoop low and give from our hearts. And whatever gift we have been granted, let be as a gift of service to others, always serving with a humble and gentle spirit. One of the sayings and vows of those walking the Bodhisattva path illustrate the life of a servant, and it is very similar to the words Yeshua spoke of when he said:

"Even the Son of Man did not come to be served,

but to serve, and give his life as a ransom for many."

- Gospel of Mark 10:41-45

His life was laid down for the release of those held captive by the suffering of this world, demonstrating the highest level of service of a Bodhisattva.

So long as the sky and the world exist, my existence will be

here for the eradication of the miseries of all beings. Let me

suffer all the sufferings of beings and let the world be happy

(and liberated) by dint of all merits of me, Bodhisattva.

- The Way of the Bodhisattva

In the text down below, the monks are instructed to go into the world for the good and benefit of all beings, with compassion reaching out to all that they come into contact with, washing them with the water of loving kindness, and helping them along this tricky path we call life.

"Go ye bhikkus [wandering monks], and wander forth for the

good of the many, for the welfare of the many, in compassion

for the world, for the benefit of all beings."

The Buddha dedicated his entire life to the cause of benefiting others, serving day and night until his very last breath. It was this spirit of service that the Buddha and Yeshua embodied, showering souls with unlimited compassion. Regardless of their position in society, all were treated with the same respect and loving-kindness, and the sick or outcast were welcomed, embraced, and made to feel accepted. As Yeshua mentioned, even the tiniest creatures we cannot see with our eyes, our neighbours, were treated with immense care and love. All creatures, great and small, have the same right to live here as other beings, and we are called to treat and serve our environment, including our lakes, rivers, seas, trees, and the air we breathe, so that every creature can feel the benefits of our loving service.

In the Metta Sutta of the *Suttanipata and Khuddakapatha,* Buddha describes how *metta* is to be cultivated towards all living beings:

> Whoever are living beings,
>
> Either trembling or firm or any other,
>
> Those who are long or huge,
>
> Middle-sized, short, atom-sized, fat,
>
> Those seen or those unseen,
>
> Those who live far or near
>
> Those born and those yet to be born,
>
> May all beings be happy.
>
> As the mother protects her only child even at the cost of her own life,
>
> in like manner is boundless, loving kindness to be cultivated towards
>
> all living beings.

The understanding that all living creatures have a life that is also precious is in several of the Buddhist text.

> Everyone dreads pain, punishment, torture, or killing.
>
> Life is dear to all. So equating others with one's own life,
>
> one should not hurt or kill.
>
> ~ Dhammapada, 130

Beloved, let us love one another, for love is from God,

and whosoever loves has been born from God and knows God.

- 1 John 4:7

Notice that it says, 'whosoever loves.' It doesn't specify whether you are a Christian, Jew, Gentile, Hindu, Muslim or Buddhist - it simply says *'whosoever.'* We are called to love all of God's creatures, no matter their caste or creed, age or wealth. This is the service we have **all** been called to, and it is the only service that can wash, forgive, cleanse, restore, and enlighten. The way to achieve this is to stoop down and wash our neighbour's feet with our tears of loving kindness, for this is the path that moves the very heart of God.

ARE WE REALLY LISTENING?

As we delve deeper into our inner practice of prayer and meditation, walking mindfully with the sacred All, we all aim to avoid past mistakes to prevent further disappointments. However, as we know, it is almost impossible to do so. Walking the inner path, listening to the small, still whispers and discerning the things we cannot see can be challenging. Even the most awakened souls will inevitably make mistakes. It is one of the certain ways we learn. But it becomes increasingly problematic if we are led by our lower desires, fulfilling life from the ego-self instead of our true light and nature. The lust of the eyes or the craving for material things will pull us further away from the small, still voice. Pride will push us at all costs to win. Trying to achieve and being highly competitive may sound reasonable and good. Still, we can easily lose control and become consumed by selfish ambition, thus blinding ourselves spiritually and leading us in a direction that conflicts with what is sacred, right, and holy: the way of God versus the way of man or walking in the Spirit versus walking in the flesh, walking mindfully versus walking blindly.

For my thoughts are not your thoughts,

neither are your ways my ways, says the Lord.

- Isaiah 55:8

The pure stream of thoughts birthed from a walk with the Spirit of Holiness is not so easily achieved. Not because Spirit is unwilling but because we have become full of our selfish ways, and our hearts and minds have become like the busy streets at rush hour; anxious, nervous and manic traffic. This is not the condition to hear the small, still, sweet voice of the Sacred One.

Most people do not believe one can be led by an Omniscient, All-Knowing, and all-loving Living Presence. But are they listening to the right things and being led by the right forces? Are they truly in a condition to receive what they need rather than what they want to happen? Are they in the right place in their lives, or have they become filled with toxins and habits causing them to spiral out of control? Have their soft, beautiful hearts become hardened and covered with thick protective layers, afraid of being hurt?

"Behold, I stand at the door and knock. If anyone hears
My voice and opens the door, I will come in to him and
dine with him, and he with Me."

- Book of Revelations 3:20

The sound of knocking is everywhere. It's in your every 24-hour cycle. It's in the living book of nature, written in the stars, the seas, and even on our bodies. Our bodies are temples and record our whole life. It's written in the tablets of our hearts, but are we ready to hear this voice that wants to come into the most central place of our lives and dine with us, commune and reveal to us that we may need to forgive someone? Or let go of that destructive habit, step out of that inappropriate relationship, or walk away from everything you thought was the truth? The small still voice, the way, the truth is all loving and only beneficial for the whole of our lives, but where's the catch, you may be asking? It's His Way and not my way; that's the catch! That takes accepting and getting used to. So, what do you mean by that, you might ask? Pray for those who hate, bless those who curse you, give to the poor, and if someone takes your phone, give him your jacket too.

Turn away from all that separates you from acting lovingly. Bless those that curse you. Let your light shine before all men, and live a life that glorifies your Father in Heaven. Honour your parents; keep your word; let your 'yes' be a yes, and 'no' be a no. Love your enemies. Give to those in need, and don't boast about it. When you fast, anoint your face with oil so men don't notice you are fasting. Judge not. Do not share sacred things with those that have no real love in their hearts for such things. Choose the narrow path away from pride and the things that pull you down. Be grateful for having a human life. Love all sentient beings. Walk cultivating compassion, love and wisdom.

As we live to please the source of our being, the voice of our Source appears and will resonate everywhere. His beautiful language appears before our eyes, and we enter a beautiful new life.

The heavens declare the glory of God;
And the firmament shows His handiwork.
Day unto day utters speech,
And night unto night reveals knowledge.

There is no speech nor language

Where their voice is not heard.

Their line has gone out through all the earth,

And their words to the end of the world.

- Psalm 19 1-4

There is no speech or language where their voice is not heard. Their voice goes out into all the earth, their words to the end of the world. This language can be felt through our circumstances, gently guiding us into the correct alignment if we need to be realigned. It can appear in nature - a seed, a garden, a flower, a shooting star, a bird, or a tree. It could manifest through our history or even our chronology.

For since the creation of the world His invisible *attributes* are clearly seen,

being understood by the things that are made, *even* His eternal power

and Godhead, so that they are without excuse.

- Roman 1 -20

It can appear as a small still whisper in our hearts if we are in the right space of stillness and ready to hear without grasping what we want.

And after the earthquake a fire, *but* the Lord *was* not in the fire;

and after the fire a still small voice.

- 1 Kings 19:12

Reading, asking, and talking about those who have walked this path before is comforting and rewarding, with records kept and preserved for thousands of years. Prayer and meditation are powerful ways of linking and demonstrating that we want to walk on this path. Our hearts and minds need to be re-tuned and re-wired, which is what happens to us in prayer and meditation. You become more attuned and aware like you are growing spiritual antennas. Prayer becomes a dialogue and not a monologue. As you tune in and listen more, you become enveloped by the very presence, and the sound waves slowly become a new language you can feel in your heart and start to understand its interpretation. It sounds easy, but it takes time, trial and error, and most importantly, becoming empty of one's small self is essential.

> Most assuredly, I say to you, unless a grain of wheat falls into the ground
>
> and dies, it remains alone; but if it dies, it produces much grain.
>
> - Gospel of John 12:24

The grain of wheat falling to the ground and dying is us approaching with humility and allowing our ego self to dissolve as it enters the presence of Stillness, thus losing its grip and hold on wanting to control life rather than life flowing on its own accord.

God is not silent. It is we who are **not** listening. But do we want to hear His voice? Are we ready to hear what He has to say on the matter? Do we want to adopt His ways when deep down we are gripping to our ways, our methods, traditions, dogmas, man-made religions and false belief systems?

There is no single way to connect to Him because, in Him, we breathe, move and have our being. He is in ALL because He is The All. And at the same time, you don't have to join the right club, church, sect or group to hear His voice. Instead, you have to follow His instructions to you:

> Behold, I stand at the door and knock. If anyone hears My voice and
>
> opens the door, I will come in to him and dine with him, and he with Me.
>
> - Book of Revelations 3:20

Open the door of your heart and allow God's love to come in slowly and direct your lives into a new life, where He will reveal more and more about His ways daily. It can simply be at home when you have time alone, to set some time alone and again open your heart to the force of love that is speaking today, yesterday and forever.

TIME TO LET GO

Before we unpack the subject of letting go, let's explore this wonderful story in the Zen tradition, to which I have amplified and added my flavour.

Once upon a time, two travelling monks had reached a town where they saw a young lady dressed in a silk dress who could not step out of her chair due to a puddle in front of her that would spoil her beautiful dress. She had been invited to her best friend's wedding ceremony and wanted to look immaculate as she was asked to present a bouquet. However, the rain wouldn't stop, and the puddle kept rising, making it increasingly difficult for her to cross. At that moment, she remembered the words of her grandmother, a gentlewoman of faith, 'When you are stuck in the mud, don't fight it, but rather accept it fully, and if you cannot get out, ask for help from our Father/Mother from whom the Breath of Life comes from.' She closed her eyes, gently opened her heart, and lifted a prayer from the centre of her soul as if a sweet-smelling fragrance of incense was released, reaching the very heart of the Universe. The two monks noticed her within moments, and the older Monk immediately felt her intention. He picked her up and carried her fifty meters in the same direction she wanted, through a street with a roof covering. The young lady ran towards the wedding location when the Monk put her back down. The Monk also quickly returned to the direction of his destination. There were no thanks, goodbyes, or any gestures of appreciation, simply the action of what was required - an act of unconditional compassion expecting nothing in return. The younger Monk noticed that the woman said nothing, not even a glance with her beautiful eyes or a gentle bow as a gesture of thanks or some form of acknowledgement for being transported over to dry ground, keeping her dress clean and dry. As the two monks continued, the younger Monk was huffing and puffing, seemingly troubled, and eventually said, 'That woman was extremely rude. She is young and beautiful, and you are an old monk who carried her on your back. Furthermore, we had been travelling for hours without any breaks or food, and she didn't even thank you or offer you some water or food. How rude and disrespectful is that!' The older Monk replied, 'That was hours ago that I picked her up and prevented her from spoiling her beautiful dress and then placed her down so she could enjoy the rest of this beautiful day. Why is it, my friend, that you are still carrying her?' The younger Monk's expectation of seeing a gesture of gratitude and his judgment of why she didn't show any appreciation kept him preoccupied, annoyed, and angry, possibly causing him to miss all the delightful places the landscape had to offer along the way. Instead, he judged her actions based on what he wanted to happen. Maybe she was the most grateful soul in the world at that moment and had no time to waste, or perhaps as the Monk lifted and transported her, she sang her gratitude to the heavens above for answering her prayer. What is clear is that the elder Monk was flowing and moving. It was an overflow of compassion at that moment, seeking nothing, attached to nothing, and expecting nothing in return. This is selfless, loving energy flowing. It moves as it should, empty of selfish desires but full of metta (loving-kindness), and this kind of love seeks nothing in return. It's also possible that the younger Monk wanted to carry the beautiful young woman himself and transport her to dry and safe ground but was unable to because he was afraid she might say no, or that he would be moved and pulled by her beauty. These are all possible scenarios, but what is clear is that the young Monk was still carrying the past on his shoulders and had become weighed down and angry. Anger, regret, and bitterness are emotions we feel when we are still holding on to the past, clinging to what might have been or could have been. They keep us from moving and living in the magic of the moment.

Most of the time, these actions are not because we want them but rather habits that have formed and become the norm in our everyday lives. But can you imagine the accumulative effect of doing this every time a situation doesn't match what we expect or desire? Anger can quickly build and transform into a rage, and we may even do something we regret later. These energies in our lives are real, and if they are not correctly handled, they can cause further harm to us and others. I know it's not so easy to let go sometimes, and it seems a lot more natural to hold on, but once you understand that holding on, gripping and not letting go is damaging to you and others, you will take up the challenge to let things rise and fall, contract and expand, breath in and out. Again, I understand letting go is not easy, especially if you are letting go of a loving relationship in which you have invested your heart and time but have abruptly ended. Letting go of someone who has hurt you and somehow feels that they got away with it and you are the one who suffered and may still be suffering. I know how it all feels, especially when you are going through it alone. But what I am pointing out to you, my dear friend, is if you don't let these things go, then the heaviness you feel will only increase, and the energy will change and become more toxic as energy transforms and does not die. Holding on to negative energies is toxic, allowing resentment or anger to remain inside you and through you can trigger your flight or flight response, affecting your heart rate and blood pressure.

But your beautiful heart deserves all the loving care in the world. It's your home, where your essence wants to flow from, not where anger, bitterness, and resentment are to be stored, which creates sickness and pain. You are too precious for that, my beloved friend. Anger only leads you to say things you may regret. You know this is true. I know we all say things we don't mean, but deep down, you love and care and want no damage done to any living creature. I know you don't mean to shout and say the things you have said. Please hear me. I am not pointing the finger but just pointing out what not letting go does to your precious lives. Frustration is also an energy that often causes us to give up on our dreams, learning new skills and beneficial things. Frustration only births impatience, and patience is required in every part of our lives and at every stage. The emotion of guilt envelops us with shame until we feel we are not equal, an outcast, ashamed and unable to live and move forward. And this, my beloved, was not the life you were created to live and experience. And how many times has fear held you back?

You deserve better than this, my precious friend. Can you see how damaging these energies are to you and your life? The wonderful news is that you don't have to carry this weight on your shoulders, hiding and afraid of what this world may say or do to you. You can live a life of complete freedom, where these toxins will not be able to cling and create a home in you, a life where you can grow wings and fly above and beyond these toxins. But to grow your wings, you must first let go of the baggage. It may be time to forgive someone who hurt you and lay down that unending cycle of pain. To forgive is a choice to heal yourself. Let go of your anger; it will only benefit your precious heart, thus improving your overall health and well-being.

Sometimes, we act like these things are not there. But the first stage in finding freedom is creating the space to look at it. Don't be afraid to look at it. This is why you have been running away, trapped and unable to move on. Because, my dear friend, you have been afraid to look at it, but you don't need to be. Imagine you are looking at your adorable son or daughter, and they are approaching you with the same issue. Imagine your gentle, loving spacious eyes looking at yourself and these issues with the deepest loving care. By doing this, you say, "Come and sit with me in an atmosphere of love and truth. I am ready to face you with love, truth and care."

This is the first brave step you have to take to break the regular cycle of running away, becoming too busy, or masking your problems. Step two in your journey towards freedom is accepting things as they are, being honest with yourself without blame or shame, and loving ownership of what is there. So, once you have completed step one, create a space for stillness in an atmosphere of loving kindness, and then take ownership of your part in the situation. Then, you can finally begin to breathe naturally. Breathe in, and when you exhale, let go of your worries; start releasing them and move forward into your new life immediately. If that means saying sorry to someone, facing a situation you've been avoiding, or writing a letter you've been putting off, then do it.

To let go – we have to be the first ones to open.
To say sorry - we need to open our mouths.
To say I forgive you – we need to open our hearts.
To see clearly - we have to open our eyes.

It all starts with creating space, the space of loving kindness, moving into ownership, seeing things as they are, releasing and letting go, and finally, walking the new life. Once you have done this, please be patient because it won't happen overnight. It's a step-by-step process, layer upon layer. It's not just a temporary fix but a new lifestyle and path that needs to be followed until your last breath. This new route is the path of letting go, and with each step, you will begin to feel lighter. That's the sign that the baggage of your past is finally laid to rest. You, my dear brother or sister, will begin to feel your heart open again with a new song. Your feet will dance again, and you will be happy to be yourself again. Liberty and freedom will naturally appear, and letting go will be as easy as breathing.

Whoever seeks to save his life will lose it,

and whoever loses his life will preserve it.

- Gospel of Luke 17:33

MISSING THE MARK

I have called this subheading "Missing the Mark" because that's probably the best translation for the word "sin". It is a word that needs to be explored and understood correctly without the connection of shame or guilt attached to it if we are going to grow in a genuine, authentic, healthy spiritual way. In Greek, ἀμαρτία/hamartia is a word where we get the word described as 'sin' which is correctly interpreted as "to miss the mark"; or in Hebrew, khata "to miss the goal" or chatá meaning "to go astray"; adhamá in Sanskrit meaning "wrongdoing, misconduct or behaviour" which are inconsistent with the Dharma, the Universal Laws.

If we observe this word and its meaning, even though Hebrew, Greek and Sanskrit are very different languages, the four words Harmatia (Greek), khata or chatá (Hebrew) and adhama (Sanskrit) all end with the letter "a". The first letter of our alphabet, so you can imagine that if this first letter is used out of point, context, or incorrectly placed, we wouldn't have any harmony or correct sentences. Things would be much harder to comprehend as they would be out of alignment. So, this is a more accurate way to understand the word 'sin' and its effects on our lives. Unfortunately, sin is a word that has been misused, abused, wrongly understood, and often connected to endless guilt, shame, and fear. Once you know and understand it, it can be a life-giving word because it can help you avoid and prevent unnecessary pain and suffering.

The way Yeshua looked at human beings living in Harmatia (sin) was consistent with the meaning of missing the mark, going astray or missing the goal and with these texts, you can feel his heart and intentions towards man:

"For the son of man came to seek and save the lost."

- Luke 19:10

"What man of you, having a hundred sheep,
if he has lost one of them, does not leave the ninety-nine in the
open country, and go after the one that is lost, until he finds it?"

- Luke 15-3-4

He was expressing here that if the ninety–nine other sheep were safe and one missed the mark and went off into dangerous territory, he would leave the safe ones and go after the one lost. When you miss the mark of your true centre, authentic self, and inner light, you are on dangerous ground because you can spin off in any direction. Yeshua was trying to express how sacred, valuable, and precious we all are.

In a previous chapter, we also looked at the teaching of the Parable of the Lost Coin (*Luke 15:8-10*). Yeshua used to teach through parables with deep symbolic meanings. The woman with the lost coin, depicted as 'female,' represents the softer aspects of who we are - our spiritual centre or heart. The number ten symbolizes God within us - our true essence, our light perfected. A coin usually has an image representing our true image and likeness. *Lighting a lamp* refers to **prayer** and **meditation**, much like lighting a lamp so we can see our way back. Cleaning our lives (*sweeping the house*) means turning away from things that harm us, repenting, and turning to life with light consistent with our True Nature and Universal Laws. When we read this parable, we understand how sin affects our light, distorts our true likeness, and hides our true image. We miss the mark of our true nature and the goal of our true light. So until we stop, switch the light on, and sweep our house from the errors we make, from all the bad habits we form that only cause injury and misery, we will never find the peace and harmony we seek.

The next day John saw Yeshua coming toward him and said,
"Look, the Lamb of God, who takes away the sin of the world!"

- Gospel of John 1:29

To understand the primary mission of Yeshua on Earth, we need to acknowledge that we were born into sin; we have **missed the mark**. Yeshua was born into this world to shine a light on sin and its effects on us as individuals, a community, a nation, and a global whole, including all sentient beings and Mother Earth. He came to bring restoration and to help us all live in correct alignment again and be restored with our Source, The All, the Father of Lights. However, we are merely touching lightly on this greatest act of God's love to bring an understanding of the word 'sin'.

The All is Love, and so is our essence. How can we have a union if we live outside The All, away from our essence? It will be impossible. There is a disconnect, as though we are cut off from the power source itself, and this is what sin does. It separates us from the same

Love of our Source. This spiritual feeling of being cut off, separated from even being aware of this love, causes us to spin in many directions, searching and desiring something that could fill the void we are feeling. But the truth is, no matter how much we keep looking, resisting, and searching, it will never be found or replaced - because the "very thing we seek is seeking us", as Rumi once quoted.

Yeshua said "Those who seek should not stop seeking until they find.
When they find, they will be disturbed. When they are disturbed,
they will marvel, and rule over all."

- Gospel of Thomas (saying 2)

And back to Rumi's saying, "The very thing we are seeking is seeking us". That is so true. We all seek to know Love, find our purpose and belonging, and feel cherished and protected. We go out searching for this experience, for this connection, for a union we know is there, but somehow have lost or forgotten, and when we return to it, we realize it was searching for us, waiting to cover us with its wings, waiting to welcome us. As Yeshua said in the Gospel of Thomas, we should not stop seeking until we find it, but we are disturbed when we eventually find it. We search in all the wrong places. Religion, pleasure, relationships, and works, only to find I was looking in all the wrong places. You may search and search everywhere, as I did. You may even search for it in drugs in long hours of prayer, fasting and meditation, all in your strength. So, when you find it, you will surely be perplexed and realize that it has been staring at you in the face all along. You couldn't see it. It is at the core of your centre, and it is everywhere too.

Split the piece of wood, and I am there.
Lift up the stone, and you will find me there.

- Gospel of Thomas (saying 77)

We are indeed the very thing we are searching for. We are the light, the truth, the way, the love, the purpose, the treasure, the worth, and the value we are seeking. It seems so easy, way too easy! And that's why we find it so hard to access because it seems too simple. We prefer to push, strive, struggle, graft, work for it, and search long and hard. I know this full well because I am guilty of this very thing. But none of it will ever help you experience the beautiful, wonderful treasure that you were born to be, that you are, in essence. It's already there, complete. You **are** the result that you have been searching for always. You **are** that radiant light spoken about, only we have forgotten and dug in the wrong places. We have learned to use survival instincts to grow up and live in a dog-eat-dog world. In a world run by consumerism at all costs, the love of money and where power rules, and if you don't quite match up to the pace, you slip down the ladder. Pushing, striving, enduring, and fighting are adequate words when pursuing or achieving goals. Still, they will only spin you further and further away from your centre and into tension and frustration. How can you push for something that you already are? You are only fighting against yourself.

So, there are only two things to do: *surrender* and *yield*. Let go, trust, and accept that you are what you seek. If you read the Gospel of Luke 15, the Parable of the Lost Coin, The Lost Son, and The Lost Sheep, you will soon discover that Yeshua was lovingly trying to call us back to our true home.

Yeshua called a little child to him. And he said, "Truly I tell you,

unless you change and become like little children,

you will never enter the kingdom of heaven."

- Gospel of Matthew 18:2-3

Yeshua challenges us to live a pure and wholesome life, close to our true nature, the nature within us that is like a free child without shame or guilt. Sin kills purity, filling our lives with destructive toxins, and what person would want water filled with toxins versus pure, living, fresh water filled with energy and goodness?

Think about how we pollute our rivers, lakes and seas and how it affects marine life. It's the same as when we pollute the air we breathe and how it affects our lungs. There is a law, a truth, and an integrity to everything. You don't expose your neck that connects the heart and brain to the wrong pillow because if you do, your neck will be out of line, missing the mark, and out of integrity to the rest of your whole body, and you will suffer some.

I want you to learn to appreciate the word "missing the mark" (sin) by understanding it as the past masters taught it without confusion. If you settle with it, it is a word that will keep your life in harmony; where there is harmony, there is health and well-being. Develop the right spirit before it's too late and before you suffer the consequences of living out of proper alignment.

I want to close with the essential thing about missing the mark (sin). The true light within you, the Presence of God, cannot and will not engage with us when we live a life of sin, not because this Presence doesn't love nor want to, but rather because sin is the antithesis of our light essence, our very core nature, a nature that wants to become one and enjoy the union. It would be the same if you had a friend that came to your house and started stealing or destroying your home, acting unruly. You would ask him to change if you had patience and a lot of love. But after a while, you would say to yourself, "I can't do this anymore", not because you don't love them but because you couldn't relate to that way and behaviour anymore. Sin separates us from this beautiful, peaceful presence and becomes a spiritual death. This is why Yeshua spoke about it so often that we would take its effect seriously.

In the Gospel of Matthew, chapter 18 v 9 says, "And if your eye causes you to sin, gouge it out and throw it away." He didn't want us to gouge our eye out, but he told us to lay the axe at the root. He encourages us to have an attitude that loves harmony and repels everything and anything that separates us from that.

A man reaps what he sows because the Law of Causation is always at work. We cannot escape this; we will become corrupted if we sow seeds of corruption. How can we enjoy the beautiful things life wants to give us, the wonderful friends, and the heart-warming and loving moments? If we sow unrest, how can we have peace? If we sow hate, how can we have love? If we sow fear, how can we enjoy life without worry? Light and darkness cannot have a union because the moment light shines, there is no more darkness. Therefore, the two cannot marry because of what light is and what it does. The light shines, and the darkness does not comprehend it because the moment it comes into contact with it, the darkness is no more.

We, too, are Light beings, called to walk in the Light and have fellowship with the Light. To walk in the light of Truth, the light of Love, the light of our Awareness. It's the only way to experience life with immense joy and power outside of sin. So, love the Light with all your heart and grow to understand sin's destructive effects on your life, and you will find harmony again.

The eye is the lamp of your body; when your eye is clear,
your whole body is also full of light; but when it is bad,
your body also is full of darkness.

- Luke 11:34

We all know that there are two kinds of eyes: the ones that see externally and those that perceive internally. We can call the ones that see externally the "materialistic eyes" and those that see with eyes of wisdom and truth (internally) receive insight. Perceiving, discerning and interpreting life as it is.

Blessed are the pure in heart, for they shall I see God

- Gospel of Matthew 5:8

Selfish desires such as greed, hatred and ignorance prevent this light of loving wisdom from overflowing into our lives. Instead, we get trapped in the lower, denser parts of the external world, following what our eyes see and lose contact with the inner eye.

This kind of life only corrupts our ability to see clearly, which is another unfortunate injury we do to ourselves, becoming trapped and gripped by sin. No amount of cleaning on the outside, following religious rituals, wearing religious clothing, or carrying sacred beads will restore one to its original beautiful light that is always patiently and lovingly waiting for its return. One has to stop, turn around and walk home. And only when we do, will the path of healing and restoration take its majestic effect in our lives.

But my dear friend, if you are reading this and feel the weight of sin pressing on you, and you feel as though you are a million miles away from home, please remember that the moment you choose to return, a blanket of love will be placed around you, covering you and ready to embrace every part of your life, with the song "My son, my daughter was lost and now is found". A ring will be placed on your finger to symbolize your new friendship with your true heart, and new shoes will be given to you to walk in the Way of Light. There is no condemnation, no more guilt, and no more shame where there is Love. You are a precious soul, deeply loved, cherished, and valued. There is one thing that sin cannot do: to keep love from loving the person, for love covers a multitude of sins. There is no point in clinging to a life of sin when life wants to take you by its loving hand and guide you every step of the way.

Sin is a soul looking in the wrong direction,
Energy transferred with the wrong projection.
A gaze that will only end up in a destructive haze,
Awhile of separation that leads to desperation.
A moment of thrill that in the end only kills.

CONTEMPLATION AND REFLECTION

"Forgive them, for they don't know what they do."

Find a warm and comfortable place to sit, a quiet place where you can be still and unwind, let go of the troubles of this world, and switch off the busyness of your life. What's more important than a meeting with your sacred heart? Sit with your spine nice and straight so that your nervous system can gently calm down and your lungs can breathe, filling your heart with immense gratitude because you are alive and your life is deeply precious to us all. Feel that you are sacred and unique and that no one else is like you on earth. You are becoming aware of your sacred breath, inhaling and exhaling. Can you feel the ocean, the waves in your in and out breath? Notice that it's breathing you without any effort. Life is living through you and for you. No effort is required as you contemplate this letter of love to you. It's written with deep care for your sacred centre, for the preciousness of your life. I want you to know that every word is written to acknowledge every step of your journey. With and without mistakes, we have all walked blindly at times and have all said and done things we regret. This letter is written from my sacred centre to yours. Unfortunately, selfish desires of greed, hatred, and ignorance prevent this light of loving wisdom from overflowing into our lives. Instead, we get trapped in the lower, denser parts of the external world, following the outer eyes and losing contact with the inner eye.

Dear beloved friend,

I am writing this letter to you because I am aware that you understand that carrying the weight of revenge, disappointment, betrayal, or abuse is only weighing you down and preventing you from living the life your heart wants to sing and live. We become strong when weak, soft, and pliable, like an open hand letting go of something that causes further pain. I understand that people on Earth can be cruel, wicked, and even evil, but I am also fully aware that this is only because they have not experienced unconditional love. In fact, the absence of experiencing this love can turn souls like this. To be honest, the lack of love can turn anyone into a wounded animal, and we all know what wounded animals can be like, especially the ones that have been unfortunately abused and, at times, tortured.

Please hear these words - your heart wants to be free, shine, sing, love, and share. And it can and it will. So, the greatest gift you can give your heart, the most valuable present, and the most beautiful touch is to forgive yourself for all your mistakes. When you first arrived on this planet, you did not intend, plan, or commit to these errors. But there is cause and effect, and we all spin out of control at times – so please, take a deep breath, and when you exhale, say, "I forgive myself wholeheartedly for all the mistakes I have made, for all the people I have hurt, and for all the hurt I have caused to myself."

The next part is to forgive those that have hurt you. Remember holding these energies in will only because you further pain. So please will you take a deep breath in, and when you breathe out, say, "I forgive all those that have hurt me, caused me pain, abused me, cheated me, lied to me (you can put a name if you want to). I let them go; I surrender them knowing that it is out of ignorance, out of a life that has also been absent of love and therefore has produced one of pride, greed, hatred, lust or anger. I release them and forgive them for their acts of blindness."

Because you have forgiven them, remember it doesn't mean they will not face the consequences for their actions and, therefore, could suffer deeply. This is why we are called to pray for those who hurt us in any way because, in the end, whatever a person sows, so shall he reap. Therefore, may we have compassion, even for those who may hate us.

May we help all sentient beings.

Your Spirit Brother.

CHAPTER 4

YOU ARE NOT ALONE

During the covid-19 lockdowns, I vowed to keep my phone on all day, not because I wanted it to ring or because I wanted to be busy, but because I saw the devasting effects of what these social isolations would do to people. I was getting calls from different parts of the world with the same devasting news that someone had either committed suicide or attempted and failed. The fear of economic crisis and the feeling of going through it alone swept the world like a tornado. I was getting calls from everywhere with the same cry, and not from people with a history of mental health issues, but people from different walks of life. The pandemic hit many people hard. In almost every call, I noticed that the underlying feeling of walking alone, without a friend, without a helping hand, or someone to be close to, was heavy on the hearts and minds of people. I knew from years of Life Coaching, mentoring and studying alternative therapies that isolation and loneliness are associated with negative health effects on the mind and body. I was aware of the greater risk of coronary heart disease, strokes, and the risk factor for depression and anxiety later on. I had read in a recent study that loneliness was a far greater health threat than obesity. So, cutting people's social connections during an unprecedented time was not going well. So, I would like to address this essential part of our lives from a spiritual perspective so that you, reading these pages, will know that there is an internal way of dealing with the struggle of feeling alone in a world that sometimes can appear cold and confusing. Who knows, there could even be another lockdown in the future, so I would like you to know that there is hope and a way, and there is **nothing** to fear.

As human beings born into this world, it is essential to acknowledge and accept that one will experience, at times, the feeling of being alone, misunderstood, or as though they are the only ones experiencing their troubles. With that, one can often feel they are walking alone. And that is true because every soul is unique and will grow and develop at their own pace and time. However, we cannot run away from facing loneliness. It is a part of life but doesn't need to be a negative experience. On the contrary, it can be life-changing and enriching if one knows what to do when facing loneliness. Therefore, the first and most important thing to recognize is that it has a part to play in our lives, and not to be afraid of it or try to avoid it, but rather as a life-transforming opportunity.

When you started your journey here on earth, you were alone in your mother's womb, unless you were a twin or a triplet, but you still formed alone. You were connected to your mother by an umbilical cord feeding you the essential nutrients to form and grow. Still, for about nine months, you were alone, floating around in the darkness, developing, growing and preparing for your entrance. It is the first stage of aloneness that you go through. You may say, "*But* I *wasn't* aware; I was completely oblivious." My reply would be, "life was happening through you, breath was breathing you, life was forming you, and you were floating." What a beautiful memory you have already stored just waiting to be rediscovered. The most magical key lies here in this place and stage in your life. You, my dear friend, were without the busy chasing running around attached mind. Your mind was calm and at ease, like a gentle stream calmly allowing life to flow, as though you were on a raft gently moving across the shore of life. There were no feelings of being overwhelmed because there were no thoughts of what is 'alone', no beliefs, no idea or construct of what you thought 'alone' was, so the state of being and oneness was genuinely experienced.

Have you ever tried doing things carefully and mindfully throughout the day? When walking, you are just walking; when eating, you are just eating; when lifting a cup, you raise the cup - becoming immersed in the act wholeheartedly as though your life depended on that one action? If you have, you would have experienced, after a while, a deep connection with the action as though it was the only thing existing. Then after a little more time, your awareness would expand outwardly as though only Awareness existed. The feeling of being alone would be cut off like a tree branch. The sense that *I* live outside of this whole universe, alone, as a separate *I* start to weaken. Because how can you be alone? The air you breathe, the sun that shines on you, the trees you pass, the wind you feel, the branches you hear moving, the birds that sing, and the earth you walk on are all part of your life and history. Every moment of every day that you live here, they are all sharing it with you, and you with them. But let's go back to a point I was making when I explained that you were in your mother's womb, developing, growing and preparing for your entrance. Here, I want us to focus on and extract the internal spiritual understanding of aloneness because this is where alone's positive and inspirational aspects take shape.

When the Buddha's eyes opened to the suffering of human existence, it had a tremendous impact on him. It was the foremost reason he left and uprooted himself from a life of luxury into a solitary life that would lead to tremendous struggle, discomfort and uncertainty. Although we are all unique, we all share some common ground; we are all bound to get ill, face old age and the frailties of it, and eventually experience death. And because of this, Siddhartha (Buddha) left his life of comfort and dedicated his entire life to finding a way to attain peace for himself and for all sentient beings. But my point here is that he did it alone, so the time spent reaching his goal was because he was alone. What about when Moses fled into the wilderness alone? Or Yeshua, who fasted forty days and forty nights alone, and after coming out, started his entrance into his divine purpose and calling, empowered for this time, supercharged from his experience and encounter, and was able to declare:

"The Spirit of the Lord is on Me

because He has anointed Me

to preach good news to the poor.

He has sent Me to proclaim liberty to the captives

and recovery of sight to the blind,

to release the oppressed,

to proclaim the year of the Lord's favour."

- Gospel of Luke 4:18

What about athletes, musicians, and artists working long hours alone, day after day, perfecting their craft, only to leave us with works of brilliance that impact our generation and the ones to follow. From a spiritual perspective, being alone is a beautiful opportunity to explore who we are and what we carry. It is a chance to work on our skills, like the Buddha, Moses and Yeshua, and it is an opportunity to go into the most sacred parts of who we are, touch a chord in our hearts and impact history forever. Our time of being alone is when we can discover we are not alone so that we can draw close to the very sacred centre of All That Is. It's an opportunity to break through all the constructs and feelings of separation and move into Divine union. It's where the soul can develop its spiritual muscles and internal language, called **prayer** in the **sacred text**. Being alone is an opportunity to experience the pure, Holy Fire that cleanses us so we can leave our past's harmful karmic traces behind. It's where we come to know the divine umbilical cord of the One breathing through us so that if everything is swept away like it was for so many people during covid, we can stand on solid ground. Being alone is a beautiful opportunity to experience tremendous insights and receive personal wisdom and comfort. Being alone is where we can discover that we are being carried and not that we are carrying the world alone. I would like to share a dear and sacred prayer for when you are feeling deep in aloneness:

You Are Not Alone

(a prayer)

O Cosmic Creator of all radiance and vibration,

The One who holds the entire Universe in the palm of His hand.

The One who breathed me into existence before the foundations of the earth.

Allow me to soften my heart so that I can open the space
to feel the one flow of life that breathes and moves through us all.

Allow me to feel your presence as a dear beloved friend,
resting close to your heartbeat until your sound becomes one with my sound.

Thank you that we can never be alone as we are inherently one, with the One.

Thank you that your life is the same life that breathes through me,
and that is breathing me.

DISCOVERING YOUR HIDDEN TREASURE

The kingdom of heaven is like treasure hidden in a field,

which a man found and hid; and for joy over it he goes and

sells all that he has and buys that field.

-   Gospel of Matthew 13:44

I would like to translate this parable in the way I feel it best describes what Yeshua was disclosing about this treasure within us all. Discovering this most beautiful hidden treasure, in essence, can be tricky. It was not designed to be challenging or complicated but because the laws that apply here differ greatly from the rules used in the material world to uncover, discover and learn.

In the world. as we move through academia, hoping to get the best results possible, that will influence which academic institution we would end up in, thus, affecting our chances for job opportunities. We suddenly take on a personality of one that has to fight, struggle, and persevere. And this continues when we start living in the ever-competing material world. Or this can often happen when our parents grow up with a natural fear of poverty and raise us with this mindset or way of life. They push out of their fears, and with this pressure, you soon adopt a way of being or thinking that has nothing to do with **who you are**. You assume it because you believe it's the right way to live. After all, the evidence is everywhere in the material world. We soon discover that we have to work those extra hours, earn that bit more to buy that bigger house, compete, and push our way through the rat race until we become like rats and all the things we never wanted to be. Only to discover that everything we have accumulated, deeming it precious, will be left behind one day. Everything we owned, everything we thought we owned, everything we gathered, everything we held onto so tightly, and everything we thought were treasure being preserved and glorified. Passed down to the next generation, are only objects with no real life in them, of no great value. Not to say, if you leave your children with a lovely home when you pass on, it won't be of use. But it's not to be mistaken or confused as your **real** treasure; borrowed objects, because they are in your service for a while, are what they are, nothing more, nothing less.

Now as He was going out on the road, one came running, knelt before Him,

and asked Him, "Good Teacher, what shall I do that I may inherit eternal life?"

So, Yeshua said to him, "Why do you call Me good? No one is good but One, that is, God. You know the commandments: 'Do not commit adultery,' 'Do not murder,' 'Do not steal,' 'Do not bear false witness,' 'Do not defraud,' 'Honor your father and your mother.' "And he answered and said to Him, "Teacher, all these things I have kept from my youth." Then Yeshua, looking at him loved him, and said to him, "One thing you lack: Go your way, sell whatever you have and give to the poor, and you will have treasure in heaven; and come, take up the cross, and follow Me." But he was sad at this word, and went away sorrowful, for he had great possessions.

- Gospel of Mark 10:17-27

This is a beautiful story of how we can all get attached to what we think we own: properties, cars, wealth, or even titles. And once we grab onto life like this, the things we hold onto hold us captive.

So, what then is our real treasure if it's not our material possessions, titles, money, fame or fortune? When Yeshua came down to earth, he used the term Kingdom of God or Kingdom of Heaven to describe our real treasure. He wanted every soul on earth to know there was another Sacred Centre other than the current rulers who rule through fear, initiating heavy control and force on the planet. Yeshua wanted to reveal to all souls that we are all sacred, all unique sovereign individuals who also have access to the rule and ways of the All. That Truth was for everyone, not just the privileged, educated few born into elite families. And this new rule, this Kingdom he spoke of, had a King, not the man-made Roman rulers of the time or King Herod, but the King of the entire Universe and all of creation. He was ushering this new Rule (Love) on the earth, demonstrating its power to the hungry, the fed, wealthy, poor, Jew, gentile, male or female, young, old, sick or dying. All were welcome to the good news of the Kingdom irrespective of color, creed, status, fortune or misfortune. He was only interested in the heart, where this new rule, this treasure, could enter.

The most sacred, pure and precious part of who you are is God's living, breathing atom; we can call this the God-particle, the part of us that is eternal, all-knowing, fully awake, complete, translucent, our greatest treasure - hidden and buried because we need to know what it is and how to access it. We may have been misled, and so we lost our way. This can quickly happen in our modern-day living with all the demands and the many distractions. It is waiting to surface and appear in its true radiant beauty. When it does, it is precise, as in the parable. We find the buried treasure, sell all we have and buy the land where it is buried so we can never lose it again. We have realized it's the most precious gift, taking centre stage in our lives, aligning our lives in harmony with All That Is so that it can have its correct rule and reign in our lives. Selling everything we have to purchase the land demonstrates how we must preserve and protect this treasure once we discover it. And this is done by walking the Royal Way. Once this eternal truth (treasure) is realized, it must be walked in our everyday lives, in each 24-hour cycle, so that this life will be experienced and preserved. This is the meaning of the Way, the Truth and the Life. The three have to merge to become one whole experience. Realizing this treasure is not enough by itself. It's a start but not complete, as the Kingdom of God is like a mustard seed that wants to grow and to grow in experience. It needs to be realized and experienced in your 24-hour cycle. Once discovered, Yeshua gives authority from the Kingdom of Heaven, which will manifest here on Earth.

> And I will give you the keys of the Kingdom of heaven,
>
> and whatever you bind on Earth will be bound in heaven,
>
> and whatever you lose on Earth will be loosed in heaven.
>
> - Gospel of Matthew 16:19

The keys are the very instruments that open the doors. The way to activate this is by fully accepting that there is nothing we can do, as nothing is to be done. It has all been done for us. It is a gift, for without The All, we can do nothing; without the Source of our breath, we would not exist. So, allowing our breath to breathe, letting our lives be led instead of driven, directing our lives by the whispers of Love and not the selfish tales of the egoic nature, surrendering into the ocean and currents of His ways, and not our ways, are the keys.

We have to accept that we are perfect as we are, as we came, at this moment in the here and now, for it is only in the here and now that we find life, our beautiful treasure, without any effort, like a child trusting in the arms of a loving mother.

> The Kingdom of God is within you.
>
> - Gospel of Luke 17:21

The Kingdom of God (the Reign of your Centre, the God-atom, the King of kings, the Eternal Sacred Light) is in the midst of you. It's in the middle part or point and in the invisible, most central of perfect harmony, the note and sounds you feel. It's in the moment. But not just any moment, the moment of primary Truth where only pure Truth abides, pure naked reality and nothing else. It's when everything hangs as it is, as it's meant to be, without interference. It's both within and without simultaneously in the most beautiful harmony, existing at the core heart and central integrity of everything living by itself. The quicker we stop interfering with it, the more likely we will see it appear before us. For it's the same central integrity that gives the flower power to blossom, the sun the ability to sustain our lives and the look of an infant that reminds us of eternity.

In closing, accepting that this precious treasure is as flawless as a pure diamond can sometimes be very difficult for us, especially when so many look at our lives through a polluted lens. So often, we focus on our mistakes and bury this diamond in the mud of our wrongdoings. And that's understandable. However, this doesn't take away from the purity of our sacred centre, which is complete and awakened light. But this diamond has been dropped into the mud of forgetfulness, just waiting to be rediscovered. Years have spun by, but the diamond hasn't changed; it's still the same perfect treasure that it always was, only covered with the dirt stains of our past and forgetfulness. Even though it's covered with a life inconsistent with the Truth and integrity of this pure stone, it's still the same and just waiting to be polished so that it can shine, be found, and radiate its true authentic purity. With unconditional loving-kindness, it waits patiently to be discovered.

We are all great treasures, in essence, waiting to be discovered. But unfortunately, we all go missing once in a while, some longer than others. This is why understanding and loving-kindness expressed to one another is like light shining into our mud, reminding us to dig and clean our lives until we return to our Original Being.

AWAKENING TO SACRED PRAYER

If we are to closely examine the lives of Moses, Elijah, Buddha, and Yeshua, we will discover that they all had a deeply merged lifestyle with intimate *prayer*. And when I mean prayer, I don't mean the religious prayers you are used to seeing birthed from a particular tradition or a religion. Not at all! But rather, a prayer aroused from a deep connection and knowing a personal, intimate loving Spirit-God who created all things living, with Universal Laws and an order. To the Buddha, this is called the ***Dharma***; to Yeshua, it was called the ***Way***, ***Truth*** and ***Life*** or the ***Sovereign Rule of God***. Prayer was a way of plugging into the very heartbeat of the Source as if it was the umbilical cord, a live link to the same light energy of the eternal power source. Without prayer, their ministries would not and could not have existed with the power and demonstration they could do.

It was a way of acknowledging their total dependency through a genuine relationship that fully trusted an intimate, Eternal Creator who knows every hair on our heads. A loving Source that stands patiently, waiting to merge and form a deep connection, not because it needed to, but because Love is its essence, and this Love loved every part of its creation. They did not pray because they belonged to a church group, a spiritual club, or some ancient tradition but because they knew that all life could not exist outside of a Creator. They responded to the prayer call because they knew the entire Universe, the earth, and our bodies were indeed a house, a place of grace and mercy, a gift. And that their hearts were, in fact, the abiding place of prayer. A place where one could commune and whisper the most intimate private details of one's unique, authentic self with the absolute confidence that there would be a response.

From the words of Yeshua:

"I can do nothing on my own initiative or authority. Just as I hear, I judge;

My judgement is fair (righteous, unbiased) because I do not seek my own

will but only the will of Him who sent me."

- Gospel of John 5:30

I can also mention a list of enlightened souls, prophets, men and women that have walked intimately with the One, and on close examination, you will soon discover the same. Many prayers and praying styles have been transmitted to us from diverse traditions, religious groups and Esoteric schools of all ages. So how does one know which are the right prayers to pray or the right way to pray? What are effective prayers versus the ones that are a waste of time, especially when praying was so vitally important to the likes of Yeshua?

And when He had sent the multitudes away, He went up on the mountain

by Himself to pray. Now when evening came, He was alone there.

- Gospel of Matthew 14:23

Now in the morning, having risen a long while before daylight,

He went out and departed to a solitary place; and there he prayed.

- Gospel of Mark 1:35

So he (Yeshua), himself *often* withdrew into the wilderness and prayed.

- Gospel of Luke 5:16

If prayer was so important to someone like Yeshua, shouldn't it be closely examined if we want to deepen our experience with the All? How much more, then, do we need it in our lives? Having studied the subject of prayer for many years with various teachers from different traditions and spending many hours praying alone and in groups, no one has left us with a pearl of more profound wisdom on this subject than Yeshua. He was the Master of prayer. So, let's begin at the very beginning of what Yeshua taught about prayer.

From the words of Yeshua:

But you, when you pray, go into your room, close the door and pray to

your eternal Abba, (*Father-Mother of all*) who is in secret (unseen), and

your Abba (*Father-Mother*) who sees what is done in secret, will reward you.

- Gospel of Matthew 6:6

The first and most important thing to note is that Yeshua encourages us to establish our prayer life in our rooms, not in fancy buildings, churches, or temples. Instead, meet the Maker in the privacy of your room, alone and away from the busyness of life. Away from the many distractions we have all accumulated in our busy lives. Private and alone prayer without any distractions was the first and most important thing; not clever words, not the politically correct ancient language, not murmuring the exact name of God, or the perfect posture with the right environment and the right amount of sweet-smelling candles or incense to further add to the spiritual atmosphere.

Yeshua was teaching something very different to what the religious teachers were teaching in his time, and still relevant for this time, too. He wanted to tell every soul that if they were in a private space and place, the One who was in private, who sees our hearts and knows our intentions, would reward us. He wanted us to meet our Creator as we are, as we came, so we can express our precious dear hearts with all the unique brilliant details that we all carry and make our lives what they are. He was trying to say, "Your Father-Mother is not interested in religious form and ritualistic practices." On the contrary, he is looking forward to hearing and meeting with you, listening to your honesty, the things that tick you off, the things that switch you on, and the things that are deeply sacred and important to you. He wants to merge with you, not because he needs to. But instead, because His very nature is Love, and this Love wants to meet with you daily, in the privacy of your own heart. But it will never happen unless you open the channels to this very private encounter, for he stands outside the door of your heart, waiting to dine with you.

So, prayer is a love invitation to meet with our Maker as we are, in the exact honest moment we are in, with nothing else required. By establishing this first and most important rule, He is protecting us from potentially losing our precious uniqueness to religious mumbo jumbo or hypocrisy, and like sheep, follow the crowd and, in doing so, lose our bright true authentic True Self. Unfortunately, this often happens to nearly every soul that follows religious dogma rather than following one's spirit and truth. Suppose we are all created to be completely different and unique individuals. In that case, prayer must be a matter of privacy, closed-door intimacy between our true life-given Maker and our precious hearts. It can't be any other way.

But there is another reason why Yeshua first instructs us to pray privately. It is a crucial part of spiritual growth. In our private times, when no one is watching, resisting the temptation to switch off and do other things helps build spiritual muscles. Here alone, we learn how to develop an intimate face-to-face union, heart-to-heart, honesty-to-honesty, naked wholehearted transparency, tender vulnerability, and expressing the deepest parts of our being. This is the fundamental prayer that moves God's heart.

We can all pray in groups or sit on a park bench alone and eat some tasty snacks, contemplating the beauty of nature, which is awesome and delightful. But to go into your room alone while the crowd are watching the next Netflix series requires some sacrifice. Initially, discipline is necessary until you soon discover His loving, all-embracing, sweet Presence, where your heart becomes a **House of Prayer**. Next, you hear and feel the whispers of your devoted Maker in the innermost part of your being. After this, nothing else will ever satisfy you, as nothing else can compare to this experience. To know and feel His love is the most beautiful blessing a soul can experience. After this, there is no discipline but running to the secret place to share intimacy, the breaking of bread, the sweet surrender and the warm embrace. Alone in the stillness of the moment, away from the noise and busy crowds, is also where we have to learn to face ourselves: our egos, the noise of our minds, the feelings of betrayal or let down, wronged, or the sense of our insecurities and fears we have. It can be very uncomfortable and lonely and is not something we are used to because we usually ignore, suppress, run away, or distract ourselves when these feelings surface. But it's the opening of all this honesty that allows the sacred presence of light into these spaces, and this is the beginning of your freedom, for you shall know the Truth, and the Truth shall set you free.

The Holy Spirit knows every part of who we are; every hair on our head is numbered, what we need and when we need it. He knows every intimate part of us with exact detail of our lives, and it's all important to Him. All we need to do is open up the channels of our hearts with real honest communication and be prepared for a response in Spirit and Truth. God is Spirit, not seen with our visible eyes but felt in every part of us, and Spirit God responds to honesty as He is Truth.

> God is Spirit, and those who worship
> me must worship me in Spirit and truth.
>
> - Gospel of John 4:24

In prayer, we must first learn to close the door on everything that distracts us or prevents us from opening the space of truth in our hearts. God is Spirit, outside of what we can see and imagine, and responds to only one language. And that language is not Arabic, Aramaic, Greek or Sanskrit. Truth alone causes a response from The All, and only this is accepted and rewarded. Nothing else. You can pray all ancient holy prayers, imitate all the correct mantras, and recite them in ancient languages. Still, if it's not done from the essence of your absolute truth and honesty, it is a complete waste of time and will yield no reward. It's also described as a *noisy gong* or a *clanging cymbal*.

If I speak in the tongues of men or Angels but do not have love (truth),

I am only a resounding gong or clanging cymbal.

- 1 Corinthians 13:1

Your transparent naked honesty moves the very heart of the Spirit, making the advice of Yeshua, life-giving and liberating. He wants all souls to come as they are, with all the baggage full of mistakes, past errors and missing the mark, our frailty and insecurities, and to wholeheartedly come as we are. There is no need to pretend, hype, or be anyone else, just as we are now, and He will meet us there. Why? Because The All doesn't want or need anything from us. As Yeshua said, *"He who sees what is done in secret will reward us."* And the reward is different from what you were expecting as most people pray for things, and when the things they pray for don't materialize in the way they expected, they miss the real reward.

Come to Me, all you who labour and are heavy laden, and I will give you rest.

Take My yoke upon you and learn from Me, for I am gentle and lowly in heart,

and you will find rest for your souls. For My yoke is easy and

My burden is light.

- Gospel of Matthew 11:28-30

This rest that Yeshua promises here is rest from the strain, burden and weight of life outside of its correct harmony and into proper alignment, allowing us to feel light, weightless, joyful and immersed in a loving presence.

"He who dwells in the secret place of the Most High

Shall abide under the shadow of the Almighty.

I will say of the Lord, 'He is my refuge and my fortress;

My God, in Him I will trust.'

Surely He shall deliver you from the snare of the fowler

And from the perilous pestilence.

He shall cover you with His feathers,

And under His wings you shall take refuge;

His truth *shall be your* shield and buckler.

You shall not be afraid of the terror by night,

Nor of the arrow *that* flies by day,

Nor of the pestilence *that* walks in darkness,

Nor of the destruction *that* lays waste at noonday.

A thousand may fall at your side,

And ten thousand at your right hand;

But it shall not come near you.

Only with your eyes shall you look,

And see the reward of the wicked.

Because you have made the Lord, *who is* my refuge,

Even the Most High, your dwelling place,

No evil shall befall you,

Nor shall any plague come near your dwelling;

For He shall give His angels charge over you,

To keep you in all your ways.

In *their* hands they shall bear you up,

Lest you dash your foot against a stone.

You shall tread upon the lion and the cobra,

The young lion and the serpent you shall trample underfoot.

"Because he has set his love upon Me, therefore I will deliver him;

I will set him on high, because he has known My name.

He shall call upon Me, and I will answer him;

I *will be* with him in trouble;

I will deliver him and honour him.

With long life I will satisfy him,

And show him My salvation."

- Book of Psalm 91:1-16

These texts instructs us to establish prayer in the private room of our hearts and with no pretence. We are to come as we are, whatever condition that may be, and open up the space with honesty, as that's the only language and energy that gets a response. God responds to spirit and truth, as He is Spirit. And we will be rewarded with the light of his presence, a safe refuge and a resting place. Let's continue to explore **prayer** and look into Yeshua's teaching when his students asked him to teach them how to pray.

Now it came to pass, as He was praying in a certain place, when He ceased,

that one of His disciples said to Him, "Lord, teach us to pray, as John also

taught his disciples."

- Gospel of Luke 11:1-2

They observed that he was often in prayer throughout their time with him. You can imagine his students closely watching their teachers' every move, wondering how he could do all that he was doing and all the miracles he could perform. In the next part, I am using the original Aramaic translation of the prayer Yeshua gives his student to respond to the question: How should one pray?

Our Eternal Abba,

Father – Mother to all,

Who art within and beyond all understanding;

May thy way be hallowed in every heart

And thine interior guidance be known in every soul,

And may thy spiritual sovereignty become fully realised,

In us and on Earth, as it is in the heavens,

As above, so below,

So within, so without,

As in Spirit, so in the flesh.

Grant us this day our bread of the morrow.

And release us from the consequences of our sins and all our sins,

As we forgive those who sin against us;

And do not abandon it unto our tests,

But deliver us from all evil, within and without.

For thine is the eternal sovereignty,

And the power, and the glory, always and ever.

Amen, Amen, Amen.

Let's look at this beautiful teaching on prayer and where Yeshua was to lead his disciples. The prayer starts with **Our** - not mine, me, myself and I. But Our with an "O" or a circle, the All-embracing interconnectedness of the 'Our'. To understand this from the first moment, we are to open our mouths and pray immediately, which teleports us to the All-embracing, interconnected One, where every tribe and tongue, every creature great and small and the entire Universe is carried and sustained.

We are all creatures from the same Source and come from the same Light. To try to understand the concept of eternity as so many mathematicians have tried and failed is nearly an impossible task, way beyond what we can define. Instead, we must accept that some things will be outside our intellectual capacity. God cannot be grasped, understood or boxed with our limited understanding, but our lives, every intimate detail, can be shared and discussed. With the secure knowledge that He who started a good work in us will be faithful to complete it. We can rest in His hands safely, like a raft, gently moved by the sweet currents of His unconditional love.

He is beyond time and space and, therefore, beyond our capacity to be measured or crafted into the image we want him to have. He is the Eternal I Am and will be what He will be. But even so, Yeshua instructs us all to approach Him as a loving and intimate parent with the complete unconditional harmonic love of both a loving Mother and Father – a warm, affectionate, supportive and protective love. Even though The All is outside of gender and what we can understand and fathom. Yeshua wanted us to know that he was easily approachable, not some far-distant God watching our every move with a hammer in his hand, waiting to correct our every mistake. He wanted us to feel at home in prayer as though we were approaching someone from whom our very breath came from, someone that we could be our True Self and walk in our daily lives. Someone accessible within and without had left His signature on all creations. He would cover us with His radiant light and wash away our mistakes, someone with whom we could make our home.

So, whether you read that translation or the one you are used to, please know that it was an outline that Yeshua himself used daily, not in that exact way, for every 24-hour cycle was different and demanded something new and fresh in the moment. However, if we further observe our 24-hour cycles, we might want to spend some time alone in a loving union, making His name hallowed as we set apart some sacred time for ourselves. We may need guidance or wisdom (spiritual bread) to forgive someone, help in times of trouble, or apologise for a wrong we have committed. There is no formula or rule in prayer other than to come as you are, in spirit and truth, and allow yourself to be led by His loving whispers. Let yourself be as naked, open, bare, and transparent about everything, and see what happens; see for yourself.

A SACRED WHISPER
FROM MY HEART TO YOURS
(From The Source of Our Being)

For I have come to lead you by my loving hand through the shackles of all your fears and the shame you have wrapped around yourself, distorting your view from seeing how beautiful you are and how wonderful your life can be if you trust my light. You have my hand, and I Am inviting you, so come as you are, as I created you to be and let's talk about all the areas of your life that you no longer see as "beautiful". This is why I say, "Come to me all who are heavy laden". Come is an invitation to you, in the condition you are in. So please do not worry. Souls all go missing for a while, but isn't it time for you to come home?

There's no need to change anything, for as we meet, my essence will surface, and my light will appear, and the things that seemed like mountains in your life will soon melt away like soft butter, melting in a warm, gentle cleansing fire.

Come *is an invitation to connect with me in a way that is most comfortable and easiest for you to express yourself. Calmly and lovingly, without any haste, I will listen. Remember, I Am eternal, and so are you. My ears and eyes only ever respond to that which is authentic, and you would be happy to know that. So please, come as I created you, for I Am not the author or creator of religious practices or the founder of any man-made rules that only cause souls to run a million miles away. I did the same. I Am the Author of every page in the Universe, every star you see and don't see, every creature great and small, and every cell and atom that exists everywhere. Those ways are not my ways - my Spirit breathes into hearts that open with honesty and humility, and your eyes will open when you let go of all your pride and the life that you think you own. Blessed are the poor in spirit, for they shall experience my ways, and blessed are the pure in heart, for they shall see me, experience me, and eventually come to walk with me. "**Come**" is a personal invitation to know who I Am, for this is eternal life - that you may know me and my endless love for you. This is the heart of prayer; everything else is a poor imitation.*

THE PULSE OF LOVE vs RELIGION

For years, I have tried to express this part to loved ones, friends, and those interested in God's heartbeat and experiencing His presence. But the usual response I get is resistance or anger. I am not here to point the finger, judge, or humiliate anyone. I am merely asking you to allow your precious heart to test every word I say and see for yourself. This applies to every soul from every tribe, every belief system, young and old, Jew, Muslim, Hindu, Christian, Buddhist, Atheist, Agnostic, Esoteric, Spiritual, or Scientific, believer or non-believer. Honestly, I want you to remain open to the possibility of what is being said because, with all my heart, I don't want you to miss this blessing that can help you in every part of your life.

Wise Men from the East

Now after Jesus was born in Bethlehem of Judea in the days of Herod, the king, behold, wise men from the East came to Jerusalem, saying, "Where is He who has been born King of the Jews? We have seen His star in the East and have come to worship Him." When Herod the King heard this, he was troubled, and all of Jerusalem with him. And when he had gathered all the chief priests and scribes of the people together, he inquired of them where the Christ was to be born.

So they said to him, "In Bethlehem of Judea, for thus it is written by the Prophet: 'But you, Bethlehem, in the land of Judah,

Are not the least among the rulers of Judah;

For out of you shall come a Ruler

Who will shepherd My people Israel.'

Then Herod, when he had secretly called the wise men, determined from them what time the star appeared. And he sent them to Bethlehem and said, "Go and search carefully for the young Child, and when you have found Him, bring back word to me, that I may come and worship Him also."

- Gospel of Matthew 2:1-8

Wise foreigners, possibly kings in their land, observers of the Stars. But without any knowledge of the Hebrew text, which is why they ended up in Jerusalem rather than Bethlehem. It was written and prophesied by the Prophet Micah in the 8th century BCE:

"But you, Bethlehem Ephrathah,

Though you are little among the thousands of Judah,

Yet out of you shall come forth to Me

The One to be Ruler in Israel,

Whose goings forth are from of old,

From everlasting."

- Micah 5:2

Now, many prophecies spoke and pointed to this new King who would bring a new way and agreement *(Jeremiah 31:31);* a King who would be forsaken, be pierced on hands and feet, but would be vindicated (Psalm 22:1-31); one who would even be born of a virgin with a name that meant God with us (Isaiah 7:14); a King that would suffer immensely as a suffering servant - one who would bear a considerable price for the sinful karmic activities of humanity and finally put an end to the horrific blood animal sacrifices adopted by all the Near Eastern civilizations of Ancient Mesopotamia, Egypt, and Persia, and unfortunately still today with man's religious deceptions. It is cruel and was never part of God's heart and plan for humanity (Isaiah 52:13 - 53:12*).* "If you had known what these words mean, 'I desire mercy, not sacrifice', you would not have condemned the innocent" (Matthew 12:7*).* "I desire mercy, not sacrifice, and acknowledgment of God rather than burnt offerings" (Hosea 6:6).

My point here is not to confirm or prove that Yeshua was the Promised One, but instead, to point out that it took men from the east who followed a star, a sign with no access, understanding, or training in religious text, to realize that a most remarkable presence had been born.

As you read in the text above, Herod gathered the Chief Priests and Scribes, the most religious ones that knew where the exact location of where the birth of the Messiah would be, as mentioned by the Prophet Micah. But did it cause them to suddenly rejoice and join the Wise Men from the East that had travelled from afar because the stars had aligned correctly? Not at all! On the contrary, Herod wanted to kill the firstborns in the area, so the parents of Yeshua departed for Egypt when Yeshua was only a newly born baby.

Then Herod, when he saw that the wise men had tricked him, became furious and

sent a message to his army to kill all the male children in Bethlehem and all

that region who were two years old or under.

- Matthew 2:16

It is crucial to note that just because you are from a religious tradition, may know the texts, pray, visit churches, watch religious programs, go to sacred mountains, and have access to the highest Priests and Popes, it does not necessarily mean that you are close to God or know His heart. These wise men had made the journey from afar because they had discovered a light, a warmth, and a presence worth leaving everything behind. But why were they chosen instead of the religious leaders of the time? Why were simple shepherds (Luke 2:8-20) visited by an Angel rather than the religious leaders with all the correct information and religious or spiritual training? Nevertheless, these shepherds believed and hastily went to Bethlehem to see the Christ, the Promised One, God's anointed and appointed as *the Saviour* of the world and all of humanity- past, present, and future.

The reason is the same today, as it was then and will always be. Our religious works, prayers or traditions do not move God. But He reveals Himself to those whose hearts are genuinely seeking. He showed the Christ to the three men from the East, Magis (wise men) who studied the stars, and they knew where and when the Messiah, the King, would be born, so they journeyed far and wide to seek Him out. God reveals Himself to all seekers at the right time.

The heavens declare the glory of God;

And the firmament shows His handiwork.

Day unto day utters speech,

And night unto night reveals knowledge.

There is no speech or language

Where their voice is not heard.

Their line has gone out through all the Earth,

And their words to the end of the world.

- Book of Psalms 19:1-4

When a soul is ready to meet with Truth and has let go of the "I" know, then The All can reveal itself anywhere, through any star, mountain or field, by day or night. For Love, first and foremost, respects the space of free will. Love never breaks entry. It watches with eyes of kindness, waiting for us to make the first move. It is our choice always to choose love over fear and pride.

Draw near to God, and He will draw near to you.

- James 4:8

The **Beatitudes** are the teachings of Yeshua in his Sermon on the Mount (Matthew 5:1-10), where he teaches a multitude of people, giving instructions that bring eternal rewards, and all refer to the attitudes of the heart. Hence, it is called 'be-attitudes.' Not once does he say, "Blessed are you for being religious", or "When you visit church, mosque, and temple, or synagogue, or If you are highly knowledgeable and can recite and speak in ancient Aramaic, Sanskrit, Greek, Hebrew, or Arabic. Or when you pray 5 or 10 times daily or visit sacred sites." His whole message was about the rules that apply in a kingdom, not of this world, all pointing to the sacred centre of our hearts. The laws that apply there are not the same as the worldly laws. Religion has nothing to do with the Presence and the Light of God. You have to observe how religion and belief systems have been the cause of many wars and divisions in our world and still do to this day. Let's read the Sermon on the Mount *(Matthew* 5:3-10), and you decide for yourself:"

Blessed are the poor in spirit,

For theirs is the kingdom of heaven.

Blessed are those who mourn,

For they shall be comforted.

Blessed are the meek,

For they shall inherit the Earth.

Blessed are those who hunger and thirst for righteousness,

For they shall be filled.

Blessed are the merciful,

For they shall obtain mercy.

Blessed *are* the pure in heart,

For they shall see God.

Blessed are the peacemakers,

For they shall be called sons of God.

Blessed *are* those who are persecuted for righteousness sake,

For theirs is the kingdom of heaven.

Blessed are you when they revile and persecute you and say all kinds of evil

against you falsely for My sake. Rejoice and be exceedingly glad, for

great is your reward in heaven, for so they persecuted the prophets

who was before you?

Now, let's observe what Rumi, a Sufi mystic, had to say about religion:

Not Christian or Jew or Muslim, not Hindu, Buddhist, Sufi, or Zen.
Not any religion or cultural system. I am not from the East or the West,
not out of the ocean or up from the ground, not natural or ethereal, not
composed of elements at all. I do not exist, am not an entity in this world

or the next, did not descend from Adam or Eve or any origin story. My place is placeless, a trace of the traceless. Neither body nor soul. I belong to the Beloved, have seen the two worlds as one and that one call to and know, first, last, outer, inner, only that breath-breathing human being.

The lovers of God have no religion but God alone.
My religion is to live through Love.
In every religion, there is Love, yet Love has no religion.

Can you hear the pulse of the very heart of Love for you in these words? Can you see that all the religious garbage we have been taught has nothing to do with the heart of Love and its loving streams flowing through our lives? Instead, religion seeks to bind us to man-made laws constantly being added to and changed from one religion to the next, all claiming to be correct and disputing over which tradition is authentic and pure or which book is the right one and which one is wrong. God doesn't need books written from our limited understanding and egoic motives when the law resides in the tablets of our hearts.

For when Gentiles, who do not have the law, by nature do what the law requires, they are a law to themselves, even though they do not have the law. They show that the work of the law is written on their hearts, while their conscience bears witness and their conflicting thoughts accuse or even excuse them.

- Romans 2:14-15

The light of God is within us. His Love is within us. His essence is within us. His ways are inscribed within our beautiful hearts. We don't need religion or religious teachers to teach us how to discover and unlock that. Sit in the stillness of your heart and allow truth to come to the surface. You don't need to go to church to do that; that can happen on a packed train during rush hour. That's why I love the way the Buddha taught the Way. He was masterful in his approach, surrounded by his time's religious leaders and groups. He taught souls to first return to stillness, to sit quietly and allow the purity of silence and stillness to reveal itself. Stillness and silence are the languages of God. What a beautiful and truly authentic place to start. The purity of stillness is where it all starts. From here, we can begin our journey into our Sacred Centre and discover, as Paul wrote in Romans, *the very Law (Dharma) written in our hearts*. Or here in this beautiful Psalm of King David, we are to be still, and in doing so, God is revealed.

"Be still, and know that I am God."

- Book of Psalm 46:10

The language of stillness is authentic and untarnished by man-made doctrines and political motives twisted by religions. Religion teaches that you have to work hard to reach God as if it can be compared to working our way through the ranks of a business company when it is the opposite. Love reaches down to us; it's because He loves us. We breathe because He loves us; we move because He loves us. Everything here on Earth serves our very existence; it's the opposite of what the world teaches us. I mentioned this in a previous chapter when Yeshua stooped down and washed his students' feet. He still did it despite knowing that one of them would betray him and hand him over to the religious authorities, who would have him killed. The Presence of Light reaches us; all one needs to do is open the heart.

Behold, I stand at the door and knock. If anyone hears My voice and opens the door, I will come into him and dine with him, and he with Me.

- Book of Revelations 3:20

Religion always tells you to do more, be more, and strive for more, the same things the material world demands, always wrapping you in fear, guilt, or shame. But Love always says, "come as you are, in whatever condition you are in, and then begin your journey from here. My perfect love will cover you, and my truth will shine a light on everything holding you down."

Religion teaches you to pray and recite the same old prayers, over and over again, as though we were parrots – but the Spirit says, "when you pray, do it in the privacy of your room where you can enjoy a heart-to-heart, a private intimate honest, *heart-felt* union, your honesty, is what moves me for I am the Spirit of Truth."

Religion builds wasteful temples, churches and mosques when the heart of God wants to help the poor that have no food, the sick, and the lonely *(Matthew 25:35-40)*. Religion keeps building new places of worship when the heart of God wants people to worship (adoration/love) in Spirit and truth. Religion keeps adding more, which is why there are over 4000 recognized religions worldwide. Yet **God is One**. Then what religion does God accept if not this kind of religion? In the Book of James, it says:

Pure and undefiled religion before God and the Father is this: to visit orphans and

widows in their trouble *and* to keep oneself

unspotted from the world.

-   Gospel of James 1:27

"My house shall be called the house of prayer."

-   Isaiah 56:7

Conversely, religion makes temples, churches, mosques, and sacred sites into a den of thieves, as Yeshua declared in the temple. Read this text again, and you will see the very heart of Yeshua and the authority and power he had in healing the sick.

And Jesus went into the temple of God and cast out all them that sold and

bought in the temple, overthrew the tables of the moneychangers, and

the seats of them that sold doves, and said unto them, It is written, My house

shall be called the house of prayer, but ye have made it a den of thieves. And

the blind and the lame came to him in the temple, and he healed them.

-   Gospel of Matthew 21:12-14

IN THE FACE OF LOVE

"If people are good only because they fear punishment,
and hope for reward, then we are a sorry lot indeed."

-   Albert Einstein

To all my dear brothers and sisters worldwide who have found themselves used, abused, led astray, or misguided by religious poisons and toxins over the years from all religious institutions, closing millions of hearts - this chapter is especially for you. I will reveal how opposite religion and True Presence are and what happens when they come face to face so that you never fall into this toxic trap and keep your heart open to the light of your presence.

Religion has filled the hearts of millions of people over decades with three of the most controlling toxins we can ingest - **fear, guilt** and **shame**. To be afraid to live and express oneself is no short of feeling suffocated, unable to move, or enjoying the space to allow oneself the experience and express life in one's Original State. It is no different than having a loving pet and keeping it tied up to a heavy chain the whole day when it wants to run and experience the freedom of running through the field nearby.

To be made to feel that you are not worthy or loved is no different than creating a society of "outcasts". It is like saying to someone, "You don't belong here because the way you were born or where you were born is unacceptable." That attitude and transference make a soul feel totally and utterly humiliated, exposed and unable to function just as they are. It is wicked and destructive. When a soul is wrapped around these three toxins, they feel they are never good enough, not worthy of love, broken, dirty, or a fraud. Shame is the foundation and chain that keeps us in the box of all our fears. It sometimes keeps us searching, begging for affirmation and acceptance, always trying to find a cure and ways to fit in and feel clean. It keeps you in a state of brokenness until you discover beneath all these destructive, controlling toxins lies your true radiant light self, waiting to live and love.

Religion has tried to keep women chained and bound, creating man-made laws that do not allow them to show their natural beauty or even their hair, which in the ancient text is described as their "glory". Why? Because weak men cannot control their lust and lack self-control. Who, then, are the weaker ones? These man-made toxic belief systems, instilled in a people and a nation, cause generations to stray further from our Original State. And what about all the child sexual abuse cases caused by the leading authorities of the Vatican churches, which then filters down to the rest of its body.

I know what sexual abuse is like. It followed me from a tender age until late in my teens. It took me over twenty years to finally find complete freedom from all its destructive effects. Just one act of sexual abuse on any life should have any institution closed down forever, never mind decades or centuries of it. And what about the destructive belief that you will burn in hell forever? Supposedly declared as a punishment by a God who watches your every move, counting your mistakes with some scales and judging your every act? How can you live and let a soul be with these chains? This destructive fear only produces more fear, anxiety, tension and worry. How will a soul ever come to trust itself this way? I lost a friend who committed suicide because he was told he would burn in hell for all eternity. That caused him to lose his mind and take his own life. He was only in his twenties he committed suicide from the anxiety and depression he felt. We all know when we miss the mark or say something out of sync or harmony. We all know some things are not right, are harmful to others and have negative consequences on us too. We know because we have a moral compass, a light in all of us. We all know deep down when we are not loving, when we are lying, being cruel, or selfish. And we know that when cruel to others, we only hurt ourselves. We know this from the experience of acting selfish and the feeling afterwards. One doesn't feel light, harmonious, joyful or even easy after any act outside truth and love. That's missing the mark. When we break the laws of Love, we are breaking the very laws of our true presence; we are going against the grain of our true image and likeness, moving upstream where it's much more stressful and tiring.

Religion divides people groups from loving each other; let's not hide this. Some religious leaders entice young, innocent lives to join terrorist groups so that they can commit suicide bombings and destroy other innocent lives. And what about all lives suffering and facing death sentences in some countries for standing up against wicked doctrines? Let's not hide these things!

"Blind guides" is what Yeshua calls ignorant minds, as the Buddha calls them. What about all the manufactured doctrines and interpretations written to fit the narrative's interest? How can it be that both the Buddha and Yeshua tried to abolish all forms of killing and violence? Yet, after Yeshua's death, religions, namely Christianity and Islam, turned to the sword when it was clear that those who lived by the sword would perish by the sword.

Followers of Yeshua were taught to pray and bless those who turned against them, the same approach as the Buddha taught 500 years before. So, let's not hide these things anymore. And I'm deeply sorry if you have invested much time in these lifeless religions. If you seek the Truth, isn't it time to ask the right questions, even if it means you may have got it all wrong? This is true humility. We have all been led astray by many constructs and beliefs passed down to us over the ages. Real growth is finding liberation from the things that bind us. One can only really do that if they are always prepared to be wrong about everything and anything in their lives, for truth doesn't need to be defended if it is true. It doesn't need to be carried by us because we are being held by it.

"You have heard that it was said to those of old, 'You shall not murder,

and whoever murders will be in danger of the judgment.'

But I say to you that whoever is angry with his brother

without a cause shall be in danger of the judgment. And whoever

says to his brother, 'Raca!' shall be in danger of the council.

But whoever says, 'You fool!' shall be in danger of hell fire."

- Gospel of Matthew 5:21-22

So why does religion say one thing and do the opposite? Why do they contradict each other? The answer is obvious: the absence of Love causes us to act through our selfish egos, thus twisting and distorting the Truth and, therefore, living in the dimension of **duality**. Let me explain - rich and poor, black vs white, Jew vs Arab, Republican vs Democrat, believer vs non-believer, Protestant vs Catholic, Indian vs Pakistani. What do all these have in common? They have fought and killed each other.

Can you see why it's a toxic and destructive curse? It is the opposite of what Yeshua, Buddha and many other enlightened teachers tried to remind us. From the beginning of Genesis, the Tree of the Knowledge of Good and Evil was the very curse. It's the biggest food and fuel to feed one's pride and ego-self. A duality is a tool and a weapon used to divide, rule and conquer - the opposite of Love and something I will discuss in more detail in the next chapter. This is why people worldwide are turning their backs and running as far as possible from these destructive man-made doctrines that create a God that seems vengeful, angry, and enjoys killing! One of the main commandments says, "Thou shall not kill." Full stop! It's insane to say, "You have faith in a loving God, but it's okay to kill your brothers and sisters". How can you then teach that God is all-merciful, blow up your fellow brothers and sisters, try to justify it with some text, and then, with another sentence, claim God is great and all-merciful? Can't you see its madness?

Unfortunately, it's still being justified today. I see it as a sickness of the ego-self and so far away from who we are, depicting God as an inconsistent, double-minded, selfish, narcissistic, blood-spilling monster. Through the perspective of 'duality', this dimension of thinking and interpreting is birthed. The dimension where high and low, rich and poor, love (selfish love) and hate, good and bad, all exist. It is the realm of ignorance. If, for a moment, we reflect on how beautiful creation is or look into the eyes of a newly born child, it is evident that the absence of loving-kindness separates us from entering this dimension of experience and moves into the lower dimension of duality instead, where the birth and interpretation of all man-made systems come from.

We are all called to love, unite, live, share our beautiful streams, mountains, and trees, and walk and care for all the wonderful creatures that share this beautiful planet with us. Not until we truly discover the path of loving-kindness towards all sentient beings, dropping our egos, and letting go of all created destructive weapons will there ever be peace and clarity.

Remember the story of Aṅgulimāla? How angry, prideful and violent was he? And when loving-kindness visited him, he stopped and let go of his sword and destructive way of life. We must learn from this very act, for not until we have dropped all hatred, all revenge, or desires to kill, conquer, dominate, rule and divide will we ever come to any real and everlasting peace. And this is only possible if we come face to face with the presence of Love within us. All we need to do is stop, allow the awakened one to surface, and trust and follow loving kindness. The real evidence and sign of a soul that genuinely comes face to face with Love is the dropping of his/her sword. Observe history; war only begets war, hatred begets further hatred, and with the rapidly advancing technologies, the weapons created will only become more destructive until we destroy ourselves. Thus, the story of the Buddha and Aṅgulimāla is so relevant for us today, for not until we have dropped all our weapons and pride will the unfailing power of loving kindness have in any space to manoeuvre with any life-changing transformative power. The truth is, the power of this Love is everywhere, closer than our very breath. It will never reveal itself in all its glory unless we make the first move and drop the hardness of our prideful hearts. We have to create the space and open our hearts to this possibility. We are the ones who need to open the channels so that love can flow.

May we stop and lay down all the hardness of our hearts and pride before it's too late!

A disciple asked the Buddha, "Would it be true to say that a part of our training is for the development of love and compassion?" The Buddha replied, "No, it would not be true to say this. It would be true to say that the whole of our training is for the development of love and compassion."

The whole practice of the Buddha is founded on the development of loving-kindness and compassion for all sentient beings. Two thousand five hundred years ago, the Buddha taught loving kindness for all sentient beings, avoiding harm to anyone, and purifying your mind/heart. Therefore, non-violence has to become a way of life, born out of a deep fusion and contact with the presence of non-violence within us. If we all take up this **way of life**, then like mirrors, we will reflect and shine this light on all brothers and sisters who have been misguided or forgotten.

Yeshua instructs us:

> "Let your light so shine before men."
>
> - Gospel of Matthew 5:16

We are all called to shine this light of loving kindness and non-violence, which is for all of us to do. It's our corporate responsibility every day of our lives here on Earth. And when we do, it will have miraculous transformative effects on all that is living. The only law required is to love our neighbour as ourselves, for in doing so, we fulfil all the Universal Laws, which is how we demonstrate that we are walking in the light, not because we have read a few verses or are part of a tradition, belief or some holy club.

The Buddha spoke about these three roots of poison: greed, hatred, and delusion (ignorance) as the critical components of all our suffering. On close examination, you only have to observe your life or family to know he was right. We miss the mark of our true light when we live in these lower states, and there's no doubting this.

So what then, is the cure for these poisons? Generosity, loving-kindness, and wisdom.

> "Anger cannot be overcome with anger, and world problems cannot be challenged by anger or hatred. They must be faced with compassion, love, and true kindness."
>
> - Dalai Lama

Compassion and loving-kindness (unconditional love) contain the complete cure, for when we cultivate and practice, our true nature rises, and the power of it acts like a clear, pure stream cleaning and refreshing our lives. And when we forget or find our pride and egos resisting this force, we sit in the stillness, dropping our egos, our tension, or busy minds and letting go once again, opening the channels for the light to shine through. And this is a lifestyle, not a religion; it is a path and not just a belief or tradition. It is not a name or a badge we wear but a manifestation of our true abiding presence. It's a choice birthed out of wisdom every day until our last breath.

When you come face-to-face with genuine Love, it stoops down and reaches you with its gentle hand, lifting you again and gently places you in a more harmonic alignment. Love reaches you through the cracks of your armour, embracing with full acceptance whatever condition you are in. If you saw a plant in the wrong position away from the life-giving sun, wouldn't you stoop down, pick it up and place it facing towards the sun so that it could receive the life-giving benefits? Of course, you would! And that's what Love is calling us all to do. So, let's choose to walk together in this.

CONTEMPLATION & REFLECTION

A Personal Encounter with Love

Please find a warm and comfortable place to sit; you deserve this. My dear brother and sister, I hope you can feel the spirit of what I was trying to express to you. Even if you felt offended, please know that I am always trying to point out that you are wonderfully and beautifully created, meaning that every part of your entire being is beautiful, precious and sacred. Every ounce of you.

Let's contemplate whether you have experienced the heavy, oppressive hand of any abusive belief, group, religion or relationship. Then I am deeply sorry if you have, as most people have. I want you to know that there is **real** hope and healing available, and I know if you are willing to trust the inner power of Love, the unconditional Love that is in us all, and allow this Light into your life. I know you will fully restore and recover.

With your spine nice and straight, please allow your heart to be filled with a sense of gratitude, even if it's because you are breathing and reading the pages of this book. So, take a few moments to do this before going any further.

You are becoming aware of your sacred breath, inhaling and exhaling. Can you feel the ocean, the waves moving in your in and out breath? If not, notice that it's breathing you without any effort. Life is living through you and for you. No action is required – allow yourself to sink into what was written for you on the next page.

You were meant to find this book at this point in your journey, so please allow the following words, and in your contemplation, to cover your life like a warm and loving blanket. It is written from my heart to yours with a sense of immense love for every soul, and *you* are one of them. I am so happy to call you my brother, sister, and friend.

My dear friend,

The Spirit of Truth wants to cover your entire life with the essence of Truth, embracing you as a dear friend. Its purpose is to help guide your life, revealing all reality; with its sweet comfort, it wants to walk alongside you, highlighting very gently the things you may need to change, drop or add. But know, before it does, it will first silence the noise of religious condemnation that says, "Stone him or her". No one has the right to expose you. But how you may ask? By the sweet practice of honest, heart-felt stillness and prayer (real talk). The Spirit of Truth will reveal that you, too, were here before the world's creation, that you have a place here, a purpose, and belong here. You are a spirit being, a being of light, one that was birthed from the very heart and mind of The All.

Take a moment to pause and chew on that for a moment.

I want you to feel how deeply sacred your life is and how one it is with the One. As you walk daily with this beautiful Presence, all things will become new; every moment will return to the sacred present - the life-giving moment. This moment is beyond duality, only here and now, only this holy, beautiful moment. The Sacred One wants you to know how to live wholeheartedly without fear. Fear has no room where Love dwells. Perfect love is the unity between you and The All, and in this Perfect Love, there is no fear. It will quickly surround your life with peace that surpasses logic and reason. As you follow the path of Love and Light, you will be covered by the wings of Peace. A new freedom will manifest, confidence to shine brightly, humility, and complete acceptance that you are loved. The fear of the old will dissolve as you discover this incredible indwelling presence both within and without. The things that used to keep you down will lose their grip as you experience the in-dwelling Spirit. Its pure, authentic power is abiding beyond the busy thoughts and emotions. It is waiting for your thoughts and feelings to become one with it. It's a process for sure but knows that the One created us to be one, without the instabilities we often feel when divided.

This pure mind is yours and is outside the dimension of duality - in and out, fall and rise, win and lose, gain and loss. These are merely expressions of life and the names we give them. But a closer look and we will soon discover that they are all part of life's expressions.

A warm embrace as you finish. May you be filled with Love.

Your spirit brother,

SB

CHAPTER 5

THE REALM OF DUALITY

Dualism describes how humans separate and discriminate things, places, people, tribes, languages, sentient beings and all other things, created and non-created.

In nature: hot and cold, night and day, large and small. Our emotions are love and hate, down and up, happy and sad. In our thoughts, positive and negative. With people: black and white, rich and poor. And the list goes on, winner and loser etc. On the surface, it could be a clear representation of reality, and if you choose to live in that dimension or realm of your own free will, that will be your experience and the daily manifestation of life. Good and evil, right and wrong, in and out, lost and found, to be or not to be, up and down like a roller coaster, or a caterpillar crawling as it moves up and down until one day it finds its wings and becomes one with the element of Air. I am not saying duality doesn't exist, and it does if you want to live here on Earth, moving in the experience of down and up and up and down. But it doesn't have to be this as another path has been prepared for us - a path that is both narrow and eternally more expansive. A path that can be walked but not grasped, a way that can be felt but not easily described. As you have all experienced in your own lives, energy is constantly changing and in continuous motion. Nothing is ever as fixed or rigid as it appears. When you feel happy, you can quickly turn sad if you have received bad news, or you could say I dislike that person, and by the next week, you have fallen in love with them. In Yeshua's final prayer, he said something beautiful before his last breaths here on Earth.

"I do not pray for these alone, but also for those who will believe in Me through their word; that they all may be one, as You, Father, are in Me, and I in You; that they also may be one in Us, that the world may believe that You sent Me."

-   Gospel of John 17:20-21

What a stunning request, revealing the very heart of Yeshua for his disciples and followers. To return to the dimension and reality of One-ness and walk away from the Tree of Good and Evil. The two possibilities here are one Earth pictured and symbolized through the two trees in Eden, the Tree of Life or the Tree of Duality (*knowledge of good and evil*). We can all have two possible experiences here in the garden of our lives, named Eden in the Book of Beginnings (*Book of Genesis*): a state of perfect happiness or bliss, a realm, dimension, and way of life if we let go of duality and move into the experience that Yeshua and all the past enlightened masters all shared and lived. You might recall that they were naked before Adam and Eve knew good and evil. Naked - signifying that they were honest and transparent with nothing to hide. They were without shame, so there was no need to cover themselves. They were surrounded by the light of The All, in union and direct communion with The All; the I AM, and they were One. This is what Yeshua was pointing to, an undivided sacred union where we experience that All is One, without any separation, and the spiritual ache of feeling separated, where there is no spirit and matter, God and man. But instead, as Yeshua prayed, The All in man and man in The All, one inseparable existence that flows with Life and Truth by trusting and letting go of the small "I" that likes to think it's in control and separate when deep down, we all know that are we one with life, that life breaths us, that in life and life in us, we have our being and movement. It is deceptive to think we exist as a separate "I" from All That Is. It's like cancer, a wicked tool to control people's lives, to put them in split groups or classes until we have outcasts and elites, top and bottom, rich and poor. How we perceive all our moments here determines our experience, so if the mind grabs and attaches itself to a fixed 'self' or an idea of fixed structures and constructs, when life moves and changes like the weather, then we will suffer more. Its how you keep people firmly fixed and rooted in the prison of their past. By creating a high, you create a low; by creating the rich, you create the poor; by making the 'white' man, you are creating the 'black' or the 'yellow' man; by creating a need, you are creating a demand, and the wheels keep spinning. That is how pyramids structures are created, high buildings trying to build and construct a privileged caste system where one is clean and the other is dirty.

Life moves in circles, with seasons, and it orbits. Observe raw physical energy, tree rings, the planets, the stars, and raindrops, all moving in circles, changing every moment of their existence. So why have we adopted such a foolish construct when the entire Universe speaks to us every moment, reminding us that life is all interconnected, all working together even when it seems it is not? It's all one vast expression of energy in different shapes, sizes, and forms moving together in one universal life flow of constant change, colliding, redirecting, and moving to accelerate. All expressions of energy we give names to, and the moment we try and grasp at it, hold onto it, put it in a formula with steps, it changes and moves. Why? Because we are never meant to grasp life or hold onto it.

Think about this moment; how can we hold on to light, energy, and life on Earth? How can one grip on to a force it cannot see yet feel, expressing itself all around us every minute? Spirit, light, energy, thoughts, emotions, consciousness and our experience in these vessels we call bodies, all the subtle energies we experience, yet we never see. And it's moving, contracting, expanding, resting, sleeping, eating, and all the other forms of expression it does. We chase it, but there's nothing to pursue; we say we are alone when there is nothing that exists alone. Everything is connected and interdependent. Remove the sun, the moon, the trees, coral in the sea, or bees and what happens? It's all interwoven, and so are you. Even when you feel in the worst condition, you are never alone. Stop chasing and grabbing; you will quickly experience life moving through you. Stop holding on, and you will start to notice a flow you never had and a lightness in your step. Fear grips and clings while life is moving. Your lives are for living, not to be put in a box of doctrines filled with dead traditions that are gone and buried, like your past. Life is to be lived. It is to be felt, fully experienced, every second of every minute, in complete whole-hearted awareness because there, you will find the magic of life where light and love are waiting for you. So, let the dead bury the dead. Drop your past. Drop the trying, the pushing, and the chasing. Allow your breath to breathe you and the light of your consciousness to lead. End this terrible idea that things are up and down, in and out.

We, my dear friend, are one. We are never alone; we have been tricked into thinking and believing that we are. The ego (birthed out of fear) will always make you feel that you have been abandoned, alone to suffer and that you are the only creature in the entire Universe suffering. How deceptive it is.

> And we know that all things work together for good to those who love God, to those who are the called according to His purpose.
>
> - Romans 8:28

To love is to trust, then faith, the invisible cord we all have, works like an invisible rope connecting us back to One-ness, our Original State. My beloved friend and fellow partner in this eternal journey, we can only rediscover our true eternal life in one-ness if we are prepared to let go of the false sense of 'my' life. This 'I' life perceives life as an individual separate from the whole. When Yeshua commanded his followers to take up their cross to follow him, he said, "*Be* one as I am one".

> "If anyone desires to come after me, let him deny himself, and take up his cross, and follow me. For whoever desires to save his life will lose it, and whoever loses his life for my sake will find it."
>
> - Gospel of Matthew 16:24-26

What does 'taking up your cross' mean? And how does that relate to us today? Taking up your cross and following Yeshua means dying to the deluded 'self' - die of the *ego-self*, that part of our lives with all its selfish desires. This part of ourselves needs to be laid down and surrendered if we want to experience real life and the One-ness that Yeshua spoke of, and this is the hardest part of all. But with love and patience, everything is possible. First, we must shed the layer of skin that our egos have blinded us with, and when we do, the veil will be lifted from our eyes. Then, once again, we will experience the true everlasting peace that surpasses all our logic, all reason, all understanding, and the eternal dove will rest on us when we understand and embrace that which is beyond the realm of the grasping, thinking, chasing mind, beyond the mind that perceives the "*me, myself and I*" life, and into the very force that's giving you the ability just even to think.

Once you experience this, trust this love everlasting, and you will experience your true state in The All, the togetherness, interconnectedness, and one-ness. For we are That which is beyond any idea that we can measure and put in a box, we are pure Eternal Spirit, pure Light Awareness that's sitting and waiting with arms of love waiting to be realized and lived through, a non-dual presence, waiting to be explored, with Truth radiating at its core and the Universal Laws of Love inscribed in its centre.

A Poem on Duality

The Tree of Good and Evil
Duality is not a reality
It's only a belief that offers temporary relief
Let me explain, and I hope it's not in vain
For in truth, duality will only distort your reality
For anytime you split, divide or oppose
you create a rule and a destructive tool
Separation only leads a generation into high and low
In or out, clean or dirty
Winner or loser
And now, guess who a boozer is?
With far more accusers
This makes it easier
To rule and conquer
Divide and collide
And spin humanity on a false ride
Good v evil

- 155 -

The rich and poor
The black and the white
A dangerous fight
The right and the left
Left and the right
This duality will soon become your reality
I told you it's insanity.
Good and bad and bad and good
That's the reason we have the hood
A belief in two powers will create the experience of two forces
Running against each other like two wild horses
When, in fact, voice and tone
Work perfectly together like an aid to your phone.
You see, first and last follow each other
Racing and chasing
Both end up pacing
Life, energy, space and time
Blending together
No different to the weather
Hot, cold, misty or rainy
an atmosphere of seasons for every year
But in fact, they are all one
under our sun.
All required and authentically inspired.
So, in the dimension of duality
We create a false reality
A winner becomes a looser
A looser a winner
Fat becomes thin
Are you seeing this destructive spin?
These concepts, beliefs and ideas
Are only forming notions of isolation
not supporting your true liberation
That's why we have the poor and the rich
The clean and the bitch
The enslaved person and the free
And that's not life

For you and me
We are all light, bright energy
Working together in a cosmic synergy
Sound-wave and particle
But let's go further into this article
The political scene in the US has been
a clear game of chess
To be perfectly honest
A huge mess!
The rise of Donald Trump has given a lot of people the hump.
This current division needs
Some revision
Both sides spinning their wheel
Not keeping it real
And now the elections
Have revealed their infections
Black vs white
Blue vs red
Too many lives and so many dead!
We are one expression of life
Breathing and being
Sharing the same sun
The same Earth
From here to Perth.
Briefs and ideas
Should not replace
Our living space
We are one race
Within one space
Elections should be an honest
Reflection of the people's projections.
May this divide
No longer collide.
We are of the One Mind
Universal and Eternal.

FAITH NOT BELIEF

Most people today still think that **belief** and **faith** are the same, so when I often say, "*Belief* or believing in something *doesn't* mean much to me". They usually look at me with a stunned look, and not surprisingly, because we often mix faith and belief as the same. So, let me explain the reasons why.

As you have lived, journeyed and experienced life for yourself, have your personal beliefs changed or remained the same over time and seasons? They have changed, of course, and will continue to as you discover new things about life. Like me, I am sure you believed in Father Christmas and, with great anticipation, would wait for him to arrive through the chimney with his reindeer. I remember being young and open when my younger sister and I would leave Father Christmas a hot chocolate and cookies on Christmas Eve. And as the years went by, I realized it was a fairy tale, a belief I wholeheartedly accepted to be true. Persuaded by this story, I used to write him notes and toy lists year after year, and often, he never met my wishes. Then, finally, I remember visiting a shopping mall and seeing Father Christmas there. I couldn't believe that I was about to meet him. I remember sitting on his lap and hearing his kind voice ask me what note I had left him with the present request. It was so magical, so enthralling. It was the highlight of the year and something I held onto very tightly as an absolute truth, as I am sure others felt the same too. But it was a very compelling and convincing story, a nice one that I loved and wanted to believe in so much. As the years passed, I discovered that many things I believed in were false. They were simply ideas that became traditions people followed, passing down these beliefs from generation to generation. We can all be easily persuaded about anything, from political, social, spiritual, personal and even historical matters. With proper marketing, you can believe Coke is a great drink or any alcohol if it is marketed and presented correctly.

Belief starts as thoughts that can turn into stories, constructs, or ideas that you have not necessarily tested through your life experience but have just adopted as something that you "believe" you can trust. **Faith** requires action before it becomes faith. It requires you to test it before it becomes **living faith**. It has to undergo testing before it can be called faith. One can *believe* in something or someone because they have been persuaded without testing. But faith is examining and allowing time and experience to reveal the evidence. So, faith is the evidence of things you have believed in but has been tested over space, time, and space, and it is the proof and the evidence of *why* you believe.

Now faith is the substance of things hoped for, the evidence of things not seen.

-   Hebrews 11:1

You will know them by their fruits.

-   Gospel of Matthew 7:16

A good tree cannot bring forth evil; neither can a corrupt tree bring forth good fruit.

-   Gospel of Matthew 7:17

Texts of great substance always encourage you to test everything before you follow or make up your heart and mind. So, test, taste, and examine everything before you know it's healthy and correct for your life. Faith is the ***substance***, meaning it's a tangible, solid presence that has been allowed to be tried and tested and has now passed the test of time. So therefore, you can say, "I have faith in it."

When you measure faith vs belief, it is, in fact, a weak comparison. To name people of faith as "believers" is a wrong description. However, you can get people who say they believe and have no genuine faith because they agree with a 'belief' system, whatever that might be. Just observe the forces that religion, politicians and businesses use to get people to believe in their ideas, policies or products. On the negative side, they will spin their persuasive lies with fear, guilt, and shame or destroy a person's credibility or product. This spin is done every day by these powers trying to convince people with their narratives, while texts describe us like so:

We all, like sheep, have gone astray.

-   Isaiah 53:6

Sheep are always vulnerable to wolves, thieves and lions in the Middle East, so they need a good shepherd to help guide them and keep them safe. Sheep also tend to follow, a characteristic we all have if we have not been trained to test, examine, ask the right questions, and allow time to reveal if it's something worth trusting and following.

We are all doing this because it is easier to follow than to carve out our walk, life and destiny. Whether or not you accept this, you are always pursuing something. You could be following a fashion, a singer, a political view, a football club, a person, a philosophy, or a dream - all very different expressions of something you have been enticed to follow. And these can also be separated into two categories - the ones you have been persuaded of without any testing, and the others are those tested with time and based their lives on life experiences. I ask you not to believe what I am saying but to test everything over time. Think about all the people Adolph Hitler persuaded, inciting them to follow him with such a destructive and demonic regime, all the bright academics, all the highly skilled scientists, and all the great minds in Germany. It's scary but true. So now, when you read the Buddha's words (*Kalama Sutta, Anguttara Nikaya III.65*), it might make more sense.

Do not accept anything by mere tradition.

Do not accept anything just because it accords with your scriptures.

Likewise, do not accept anything merely because it agrees

with your preconceived notions.

I was as guilty as everyone else in following things. I was too young to understand, inexperienced and easily misguided; other times, I was afraid not to fit in and get rejected by peer pressure, primarily when at school and college, a lot of the time because I had very little confidence in my ability to actualize what was valid. I had yet to establish and form the habit of sitting still and asking the right questions with the right attitude. You see, you have to be in a position of absolute humility, prepared to listen to the things you may be running away from, but it might be precisely what you require for your journey ahead. Faith is like the truth that has been walked and tested over a period that has become a way of life - The *Truth*, *Way* and *Life*. Or the **knowledge** that has been understood through life and has become living **wisdom** based on experience, not just information acquired over the internet or borrowed from a book you have read. I have come to know this threefold cord, and faith is something that I will discuss in a much deeper way in the next chapter. For now, I hope you can see the difference between the two: ***faith and belief***, and the importance of examining, allowing time for testing, and finally, the sacred space in your life to establish this way and cement it in your 24-hour cycle, especially with the ever-increasing demands on all our lives and the fact that we are far more persuaded and vulnerable when we are over-busy, stressed, over-active, for it is in those moments that we lose the true light of our awareness. So, making time for meditation, contemplation, and prayer places your life in a protective circle.

THE THREE-FOLD CORD OF FAITH

As I have come to know and experience genuine faith, I will not explain it as most religious circles explain what faith is. If you have your opinion or view, please remain open if you have gotten this far in the book. And remember, always test everything you are taught with humility and patience.

In the Pali language of the original Buddhist texts, faith is **Saddha** - translated as trust or confidence. However, the literal meaning of *Saddha* is to place your heart upon it. In other words, directing our hearts over to a specific alignment. In Sanskrit, the term is bhakta - describing someone's loyalty, devotion and faithfulness. In Hebrew, the word for faith is **Emunah** - based on the word Em (mother). Like a mother nurturing her child, the most natural thing mothers do, as Saddha describes in the Pali, is like a mother directing her heart upon a child, giving with **Bhakta** (in Sanskrit), meaning devotion, loyalty and faithfulness. In Greek, the word is **Pistis**, the noun and Psitueo, the verb meaning to be firmly assured, with a firm conviction and dedication. So, if we knit these together, we have a clear picture of someone who is focused, confident, faithful, and convinced by a completely natural force, as natural as a mother nurturing her child with her heart set upon and aligned with the child's direction. From this description, you will have a much better understanding, a more holistic understanding of faith and not just how it's often taught to believe or trust. It is much deeper than that, far more beautiful and natural if we allow this incredible invisible cord to be directed and rest upon in its proper place.

The most famous text ever written about faith is Hebrews 11 - described as the **Hall of Faith**, a collection of heroic acts by everyday people like you and me, giving examples of their life's exploits. The Book of Hebrews 11:1-39 goes through the chronology of the main characters in the Bible, listing their acts of faith and linking faith with action, exactly how Yeshua's student, James, explained it:

> What does it profit, my brethren, if someone says he has faith but does not have works? Can faith save him? If a brother or sister is naked and destitute of daily food, and one of you says to them, "Depart in peace, be warmed and filled," but you do not give them the things which are needed for the body, what does it profit? Thus also, faith by itself, if it does not have works, is dead.
>
> - James 2:14-17

Faith, an internal conviction that is steadfast and focused, leads to actions, or even mighty exploits, as Hebrews 11 points out. But where is this conviction birthed from? Where is the force coming from? And here, I would like to explain the three-fold cord of faith. In a previous chapter, faith worked as though it was an invisible link in our lives - the thread that acts as an invisible alignment that allows the very life of the Spirit to flow through us so that on Earth, as it is, heaven can be manifest in our lives.

But without faith, it is impossible to please Him, for he who comes to God must believe that He is and that He is a rewarder of those who diligently seek Him.

- Hebrews 11:6

No faith, no link. No link, no life. No life, no truth. No truth, no way. No way, no power. If your body was not aligned correctly, let's say you woke up one morning and your neck was entirely out of its correct alignment, would it not affect the rest of your body? What happens to your hips is wrongly aligned; it affects how you walk, your balance, your spine, your nervous system and so on. Everything is connected; the Law of interconnectedness is working everywhere. Or if the sun was five degrees off where it should be. Everything has a correct alignment, especially our spirits. So, how much more would our lives flow if we find central alignment? But it has to come from a place of humility, and it's not something we can force or have to work for or strive to get. But rather, an experience of turning our hearts in the right direction and opening them. Something is realized when the soul truly wholeheartedly acknowledges that the breath it breathes, its entire existence is pulsating because a Creator, a creative Living Force that created and designed the whole Universe, and our tiny lives are mere sparks of light that have come from this Eternal central point. Look how Yeshua describes in the Gospel of Thomas:

Yeshua said: If they say to you: Whence have you come? Tell them: We have come from the light, the place where the light came into being of itself. It [established itself], and it revealed itself in their image. If they say to you: Who are you? Say: We are his sons, and we are the elect of the living Father. If they ask you: What is the sign of your Father in you? Say to them: It is movement and rest.

- Gospel of Thomas (saying 50)

Hebrews 11:3 speaks about faith, in that God created the Universe at His command so that what is seen is not made out of the visible. So, let's take our tiny lives out of the equation and step into God's Universal Mind. Both texts (Gospel of Thomas and the Book of Hebrews) invite us to open our eyes first and rest because we are all in the cosmos. After all, He sent forth His Word through sound vibration. And as the sound moved the light, the whole history of the Universe was created, formed, fashioned and established, as though by a mystical hand through a Primordial Creative Mind weaved its unseen, hidden magic and all the quarks suddenly formed protons and neutrons, placing and timing every micro and macro light atom in their exact perfect place.

Along with all the other elements required for all life to exist in this vast ocean we call the Universe. Life is not in our own hands like our tiny egos like to think. Our lives are not in our small over-worried ideas that we think about; our lives are carried perfectly interconnected and alongside the whole. When they are allowed to be carried and breathed through, faith arises naturally, as though the invisible cord appears. The place where the seed of faith can be watered and allowed to grow. Faith is a threefold connection, and the first connection is to accept that all life, including our tiny little lives described as a mere vapour, is not ours, and neither does it belong to us. We have been in a co-working union from the beginning; only that cord has been broken from our selfishness, greed, ignorance, pride and lusts. For it is in Spirit that we have our life; it's in The All that all came to be. All this beauty, all this life, and exact physics, chemistry, and biology to construct and uphold this finely-tuned Universe. God created it with His super mind and placed it all together in exact proportions.

That was His majestic handiwork; all these perfectly timed structures in all life happened out of nothing. And when we step back and acknowledge the work of his hands, we marvel at the beauty of all life, from the tiniest creature, the stunning peacock, the smiley dolphin, the brave monarch butterfly, or the fat bumblebee, which can lift off despite its frame.

The first connection is allowing ourselves to trust and let go. Allowing our lives to return to their rightful place as the trees let go and drop their leaves in winter, we too have to drop our pride and ignorance and fall into the hands of All that is the All that was and the All that will be. Please don't wait like so many souls I know until their last breaths. Now is the time of your liberation in the dimension of Faith, not tomorrow or next week.

So, the first connection is trusting that our lives have an author and finisher. Faith makes the first move from a response that all life is be held and knit together and not a step from some persuasive sermon you have heard or a motivational speaker. It's a response to your search, from your enquiry. So, if you are hearing this challenge today, please don't harden your hearts. The All is not looking for you to be religious. He says, "*Come* as you are". We have to take the first steps. For those that draw near to me, I will draw close to them. That's a promise! You can let go; He is holding the entire Universe in His hands; you can truly let go of trying to be anything, for your being is being breathed.

The second cord is trusting that He is in you - His image, nature, ways, and laws are in your DNA. So, being aware of The All everywhere and then of The All inside. And when these two forces form a union in the central meeting point of the here and now, in this very moment, faith becomes an action, a living, breathing life manifestation. Faith becomes a union, a connection, a relationship, not some dead religion. And your experience of these most beautiful blessings can grow, mature and become like the tree planted in the most magical soil of God's love, bearing fruit in and out of season on Earth (my heart) as it is in heaven, in the here and now. And like all those you read about in Hebrews 11, you too will do remarkable exploits, and your actions will overflow your union.

My dear friend, please don't miss this wonderful blessing. I did. Suffering, pain and pride kept me gripping until I finally let go of all the fighting, trying, pushing, holding on, and giving up. Convinced that I had to fight for it to earn it, fasting, praying and meditating for hours, using this exact mechanism with everything else in my life. I had no idea that, in His dimension, this was not necessary. The material and dualistic mindset blinded me. So, when I eventually awoke to His gentle, loving hand that was always there, I found deep rest.

I had lived a life of not trusting in The All. Though sincere, I couldn't see it; I must admit I was sincerely wrong. I had heard this trust: let go, sink in, relax, trust, have faith thousands of times, but I couldn't accept it was this easy, as everything I had accomplished on Earth was birthed from hard work, discipline, and repeating again and again. My earthly father had also instilled in me that if I didn't work my socks off, I would become an utter failure, a homeless beggar that could never function or raise a family. I had unfortunately received a transference of his fear, for when he was at the tender age of only five years old, he lost his loving father and thus lost the sole financial provider in his household. This fear had dominated his life and has now transferred to me, along with the intense feeling of being dirty after years of sexual abuse. I couldn't trust that it could be that easy, just trusting, letting go and allowing God to flow into my life. I needed to do something, which had to be more than this. It had to require more effort and force. Well, I was wrong, and in one single moment in my life, when a tiny bird had visited me, and we danced together without any effort, a bright light switched on inside of me, and this was a truly magical page that would open up the most beautiful life that since then has been a wonder, a wonder that I would like to share with all sentient beings.

"Life is like a harp string, and if it is strung too tight, it won't play; if it is too loose it hangs, the tension that produces the beautiful sound lies in the middle."

- Buddha

This **Middle Way** is another way of looking at the threefold cord. The most central alignment is when a soul returns to its correct central position. The threefold cord of your life in The All, and The All in you, and in this very moment is where the real magic happens. The tune of your life can be in perfect harmony, and you can play the music that sends ripples of beautiful harmonies and melodies. And when you are slightly off-tune, you all have to do is return to your centre. No stringed instrument wants to break its strings, but if they fail, a masterful craftsman with gentle hands knows what to do to restore it.

In the life of Yeshua, you will see how he lived without ever failing, never broke a single string, and yet he had all our human tendencies. You will see the threefold cord working without interference. So, the power of God flowed through him without measure is the reason why one of the greatest prophets who ever lived said in the *Gospel of John 1:27, "I baptize with water; but among you stands one whom you do not know, even he who comes after me, the thong of whose sandal I am not worthy to untie."*

There is so much more I can write about this, but to end this part, let me say, "He stands among us", but don't take my word for it, do your research and test it for yourself.

STEPPING INTO THE INVISIBLE

While we look not at the things which are seen but at the things which
are not seen: for the things which are seen are temporal; but the things
which are not seen are eternal.

- 2 Corinthians 4:18

A lot of people have mistaken this text to include things that they want to happen that are not yet visible, like a new job that you are trusting for, or a new house, or a new relationship, and even though they are all in the realm of the unseen and people's exploits have been written about describing faith as an action, this text is not talking about having faith for things in the material world. But instead of focusing on our alignment, fixing our eyes, concentrating our focus on communion, a union-based relationship that is eternal. Everything else is temporary and will surface and move on. No matter how hard we grip those things, they will change in the material world. Yeshua gives instructions to his students:

Therefore I say to you, do not worry about your life, what you will eat;
nor about the body, what you will put on. Life is more than food,
and the body is more than clothing."

- Gospel of Luke 12:22-23

He continues to explain:

"Rather be concerned about his kingdom.
Then these things will be provided for you."

Yeshua's teachings were very clear on this subject, and I would encourage you to study them as he gives keys that can unlock the spirit realm to those who do what he says. He goes on to say:

But seek first the kingdom of God and His righteousness,

and all these things shall be added to you.

- Gospel of Matthew 6:33

Yeshua knew that chasing money, fame, job security, relationships, food concerns, drink, or even clothing, can lead to being stressed, tense, and anxious, which can be detrimental to our health. Not because he didn't want us to have them, but because there was a much better way of living without getting trapped, distracted, and putting your heart under unnecessary stress and heartache. He knows we need them; otherwise, we wouldn't require food and have these bodies, but he wanted us to allow them to flow from a different position naturally. Notice he said, "and all these things will be added to you." So we don't need to worry, fight or kill ourselves over such things. There is a much better way, a way that is not how most live their lives. There's nothing wrong with enjoying the material world, but don't waste your life chasing it, as you will miss all the other amazing things life offers. There is harmony and balance. It requires a soul to step into the realm of the invisible, and as I discussed in the pages before, it will need faith, not belief. A confidence that stems from an inner conviction based on testing and closely examining so that you can all have a living experience and not a mental persuasion. Remember, the Pali word for faith is Saddha, which translates as "to place our heart upon." In other words, to direct our full attention, awareness, and mind focus in a specific direction:

For where your treasure is, there your heart will also be.

- Gospel of Matthew 6:21

What we value the most is what we focus on, chase and fight for. But what Yeshua is teaching here is if you are chasing the wrong things, it's a complete waste of time.

For what shall it profit a man if he shall gain the whole world and lose

his own soul? Or what shall a man give in exchange for his soul?

- Gospel of Mark 8:36-37

When we take our last breath, all the earthly treasures won't matter. All that you have accumulated in your lifespan will all be left behind. What then? Isn't it better to fix your gaze on eternal matters? Of course, everyone wants to live a happy, healthy, contented, and peaceful life. We all need food and drink, clothing and shelter, family and friends, that's all very clear, and we have those things to enjoy fully, things that don't harm us or those around us. But there is another realm of existence beyond the five senses and our natural human needs. This realm is invisible. And because we cannot see, hear, taste, touch, and smell with our natural senses, it requires something deeper to enter this realm. It requires trust, a connection, a link, and a step into the invisible. And what is the invisible? It is described as the Kingdom of God, the Way, the Dharma, the Truth, and the All. So where does everything flow from in your life? We would all agree that it is first birthed from one's mind, where everything is conceived.

For as he thinks in his heart, so *is* he.

- Proverbs 23:7

Verse 1:
The mind is the basis for everything. Everything is created by the mind and is ruled by reason. When I speak or act with impure thoughts, suffering follows me as the wheel of the cart follows the hoof of the ox.

Verse 2:
The mind is the basis for everything.

- Dhammapada

Keep your heart-mind with all vigilance, for from it flow the springs of life.

- Proverbs 4:23

When we speak of the mind, we understand there are two minds. The ancient text describes this carnal mind seeking temporary things, also defined as the mind of the flesh; the other as the Mind of Light, or Mind of Christ, and this mind seeks eternal things. The Greek word for "mind" offers a better description: **Phroneo**, meaning to be absorbed with something or to focus sharply on something as though one's whole life depends on it. Where the mind goes, one usually follows unless you learn how to observe your thoughts and allow the unhealthy ones to pass through, like clouds that pass and eventually dissolve. This is why we are called to watch (see/observe) and pray. Sit in the stillness of eternal light and allow all the soul-destroying thoughts to rise and fall. We cannot control these streams, but we can undoubtedly calm the waters of our busy minds to allow the true Mind of Light (Mind of Christ) to rise within us so that we can see what is 'healthy' or 'unhealthy'.

> Watch and pray, lest you enter into temptation.
> The Spirit indeed is willing, but the flesh is weak.
>
> - Gospel of Matthew 26:41

Yeshua instructs, firstly, to watch. To watch what exactly? It is to watch the flesh, the carnal mind, the ego mind, and the selfish ways that pull us in a different direction, contrary to where the Mind of Christ wants to lead. Otherwise, he wouldn't have added the potential of falling into temptation. The power of stillness, sitting in the Light of the presence of The All and allowing the Light to expose and shine on what is corrupt or corrupting us and others, is the most important aspect of spiritual growth. This Light will reveal the lower nature, the ego-self. When you see it for what it is and know what feeds this ego-self, you can stop feeding and nourishing it. You will begin to notice how much lighter you'll feel, how easy it is to pray, and how the effects will be felt within you when you pray. The things you see, the things you think, the choices you make, the things you say, your alignment, and your health will all be affected. A new overflow will spill through and out of your life from this place and flow rivers of living water out of your bellies.

So, entering and stepping into the unseen is all about stepping out of one weighty, anxious, worried, tense, busy mind and discovering the Mind of The All that exists in All, both within and without. But it requires us to trust from genuine experience, not mere words or other people's experiences.

When we sit in stillness and nothing else, we return to innocence, trusting the moment to appear without manipulating, directing, or controlling the space. We return to the pure, straightforward, child-like faith without overthinking every move and thought. It's loosening all gripping and letting go of tension. It's returning to the essence, the part that wants to touch and move you with its loving and deeply caring whispers. Yeshua alludes to this when he says, "do not worry..." but instead, return your attention, your wholehearted awareness to knowing your mind. Please keep your eyes on the things above that you don't see because as soon as you see something with your earthly eyes, it's already put in a box of intellectual reasoning and judgment and, therefore, no longer becomes what you see. We must allow the real awakened Mind of The All, the space it requires to shine its light through and out of us. So much religious jargon has been written about these beautiful, excellent possibilities in our lives that nowadays, people run away from them rather than running to them, making it appear as though it is weighty, boring, hard and religious. And it can't be more the opposite! It is waiting to shine and prosper your life.

In closing, I would like to leave you with this story that best describes the last three sub–chapters on **Faith** and **Stepping into the Unseen**. It is the story of a student of Yeshua named Peter, who demonstrated faith as he followed the commands of his teacher but then lost it because doubt crept in.

Immediately Jesus made His disciples get into the boat and go before Him to the other side while He sent the multitudes away. And when He had sent the multitudes away, He went up on the mountain by Himself to pray. Now when evening came, He was alone there. But the boat was now in the middle of the sea, tossed by the waves, for the wind was contrary. Now in the fourth watch of the night, Jesus went to them, walking on the sea. And when the disciples saw Him walking on the sea, they were troubled, saying, "It is a ghost!" And they cried out for fear. But immediately, Jesus spoke to them, saying, "Be of good cheer! It is I; do not be afraid." And Peter answered Him and said, "Lord, if it is You, command me to come to You on the water." So He said, "Come." And when Peter came down from the boat, he walked on water to go to Jesus. But when he saw [e]that the wind was boisterous, he was afraid; and beginning to sink, he cried out, saying, "Lord, save me!" And immediately Jesus stretched out His hand, caught him, and said, "O you of little faith, why did you doubt?" And when they got into the boat, the wind ceased.

- Gospel of Matthew 14:22-32

-

The pure Mind of The All that is non-discriminative, able to discern reality with any unjust distinction, that is non-gripping or attached to anything from its past, present, or future but relatively free to flow with the everchanging currents, Not holding on to any fixed constructs, false idols that are lifeless, but one that sees with beauty, harmony, and balance despite the raging winds and storms in our life calling Peter to come: "Come, Peter, as I love you deeply; Come Peter, because I have always loved you; Come Peter, because I created you and formed you in your mother's womb and was mindful of every detail that makes you unique; Come Peter, because the waters I am walking are not based on my efforts, for I can do nothing apart from the Father, we are one. He is in me, and I am in him; Come Peter, you can let go, my son/daughter. I have you in the palm of my hand; Come Peter, let go of this life, let go of all the past, let go of the things that have caused you to feel cut off and separated from Presence, the spiritual death, and vacuum that you have felt; Come Peter, and let go of the trying, for this is my job to cover you, forgive you, love, and support you, but you need to let go. It is not your job. It's mine. You are getting in the way, my son. Trust me, Peter. Come Peter, but watch the wind of your thoughts, for they, too, carry weight, and if you listen to them, you will end up following them and spin out of your correct alignment; Come Peter, keep your eyes on me. The things above are eternal, come on, Peter, you have been with me for a while now, so trust and let go. But if you do fall, my love will still be there to raise you. My light is always to raise you up and never to keep you down; for where I Am, I also want you to dwell. So, let's stay here together, for my desire is for you to be one, and this was always my desire. I never created you to be double-minded and afraid, so let me walk with you. I promise your experience here will be far more exciting, fulfilling, and internally rewarding. Let go, Peter, and trust me, let go of everything that separates us. Let go of everything that causes you to miss this mark. I never force you into areas you don't want to go, that's not me, but I encourage you to go to places that will challenge you for sure, for this is how you will grow in your faith and is where the best pages from your book of life are written. This mind in me wants to lead your life the same way, to see through all the confusion, find solutions, and find balance and the correct harmony in every choice and situation you must make; Come Peter, why did you doubt? Why did you fear? I have been with you always, and you are with me. Only you have forgotten. Your life and your name were established before the foundations of the earth. You were always in my heart and mind, but you have forgotten this. So let this mind be in you always, for I will never leave or forsake you."

When you re-read this part, place your name instead of Peter's. Can you feel the invitation to step out of the rickety boat of your mind and into the Mind of Christ, the pure Universal Mind? What are you waiting for?

We suffer and have suffered enough. Even with all the latest technologies and advancements, that's not a fast boat. We all know it's frail, and the storms here on our planet are rising. We have all seen the damage we are causing ourselves and all living creatures. We have observed increasing tides and violent storms in unexpected places. This boat we have trusted in is failing, and there is another boat we are invited to step into, not alone, but with the mighty, loving hand of Presence. Can you hear the call to come? To come as you are with all your distrust, feelings of not feeling good or worthy enough, and baggage you have accumulated, rotten, rusty, old, and lifeless? You will know by now that the world will always keep seeking more and more material and go to all lengths to purchase it, claim it and even go to war for it. But it's never enough, and humans are made to feel insufficient.

*But I love you as you are the only one I desire to draw close to, which means cleaning. What person wants to live in a house filled with toxins, dirt, and all the other things attracted to that and follow it? Come, not with your little feet. Make a splash, and come with your **whole** life. Please stand up and allow me to see your face, and let's exchange deep and intimate words. Come, for I deeply care for you. All this can be done just as I instructed, in the privacy of your own home. Lock the door, step into me, step into my presence, and you will see that my plans have never been to harm you but to prosper you. Test and see for yourself.*

Do you hear the voice of the small still whisper, the loving shepherd who leads his flock say, *"Whom shall I send? And who will go?"* I have heard it deep within me, covered and surrounded by the loving texture it always has. I have felt it in every cell of me, and I responded and said, *"I want to glorify you. I want my life to merge with yours; I am weak but willing. So here I am dressed in this earthen vessel, with all my weakness and frailties, but I will go as I know you are love. So here I am, send me."*

The next chapter will continue our journey into small, still whispers of the beautiful inner voice.

THE INNER WHISPER

I have inscribed you on the palms of My hands.

- Isaiah 49:16

Faith is the invisible line connecting us to what we don't see, allowing us to walk and be led by that which upholds the entire Universe, including us, in the palm of its hands. If we pause to contemplate the text *"inscribed in the palm of my hands,"* I am reminded why people would get something engraved on their skin. Think about a tattoo that people get on their skin, usually to remind them of someone they love, someone significant to them, and they want to think about it often and tell the world about it. And hands are a part of the body that we can easily see, and they are the parts we most use to touch, greet, embrace and share affection with. Can you hear the whisper, *"I have inscribed you in the palm of my hands so that I can see you right in front of me, and I can watch over you as I always have you in my heart and thoughts?"* I quote this text because it expresses how close our Maker is to us. But the real question is, how close are we to Him?

Faith plays a crucial role in our lives because it is the dynamic force that draws us back into that intimate position of being carried, held, and led, cherished, loved, and protected. We are engraved and inscribed forever in His hands. And it's unfortunate when we live not seeing this eternal imprint. So how do we grow and develop in this majestic connection that allows us to feel all these benefits and ultimately rest peacefully in His hands? We will explore answers to this vital question in this chapter.

RHEMA AND LOGOS

In the New Testament book of Romans, we are given the most important keys to the development and progression of *Faith*:

Faith cometh by hearing and hearing the Word.

- Romans 10:17

What word is the writer, Paul (an Apostle of Christ), talking about here, because there are two primary Greek words translated as the WORD. The first is **LOGOS**, referring principally to the inspired word of God and to Yeshua, who is the living Logos. The Word (*Logos*) became flesh, incarnated and dwelt among us.

In the beginning, was the Word (logos), and the Word (logos) was with God,

and the Word (logos) was God.

- Gospel of John 1:1

That word, sound vibration, and command caused all that is to be.

By the word of the Lord, the heavens were made,

And all the host of them by the breath of His mouth.

- Psalm 33:6

The second primary word is what Paul was referring to when he said, "Faith comes by hearing and hearing the word (*Rhema*). **RHEMA** is the *spoken word*. A "*Rhema*" is a word that speaks to you personally and directly. It could be a word of warning, a word of advice, a word of correction or a direction that carries a specific application to your very personal need. I would like to share some of my personal experiences with the inner voice I will never forget, and I hope you will better understand what a secret word (*Rhema*) is and how essential it is. I have grown to trust it the most, especially in the current world of mass media and misinformation sharing and the control of it all. Never has a more critical time in our history to turn to the *Logos* and the *Rhema* than now!

MY PERSONAL ENCOUNTERS WITH THE INNER VOICE

Once, I was walking on my way to meet my wife, Laarni, who was working as the Fitness and Studio Manager at a health club in Richmond. Walking towards a pedestrian crossing, I heard an unmistakable inner voice instructing me to walk slowly. In a moment of uncertainty, I stopped walking, and it spoke again, more explicit this time, "walk slowly!" so I did. As I approached the crossing, a man driving his car slammed his foot on the accelerator instead of the brakes and crashed right into the middle island of the pedestrian crossing. I know he would have knocked me over had I not obeyed the voice, slowed down, and would possibly have been killed or even maimed. It's not the first time this has happened, but many times over, allowing my faith to grow as I listened and obeyed.

Another time, two of my friends locked me in the back of a private garden we had walked into during a country walk. Closing the garden fence behind them, who were in front of me, a big brown-black Dobermann guard dog came running towards me, growling as he stood three feet away and about to launch at me. Immediately I heard the inner voice say, *"Put your head on the ground,"* not the first and wisest thing you would think to do with a growling Dobermann, right? As soon as I responded to this word (Rhema), the dog instantly stopped, cried, and ran off, to the surprise of my two friends.

On another occasion, a very close friend and another martial art student were sparring in a class I was giving. One student, about 15 kilos heavier and taller, landed on the arm of the smaller and lighter training partner, dislocating his elbow. The arm was hanging off its socket. I looked at him, whose face had turned as pale as the moon, and I looked at his arm, unable to touch or move it in any way or direction because of the pain he was in. The small still voice said to me, "blow on it," not something I would typically do, but I did as I was instructed. I decided to drive him to the hospital to get it seen. As we neared the hospital, he told me his arm was on fire. He explained it like warm liquid was running through his arm. At that point, I didn't connect the blowing of the arm and the Rhema word. I sat with him at the A&E and eventually got seen and had some x-rays done. When they finally returned with the results of the x-rays, there was nothing wrong with his arm!

Let me be clear; I have no power to do any of this myself. None of it is by my strength. I merely listen and obey, and IT does it. If it were not for the Breath that breathes me and gives me life, I wouldn't even be here writing this book. I can do nothing. Zero, without God. I do not share these stories to point to me or glorify myself in any way, shape or form. From the core of my heart, and please hear me, it is ALL God. I merely asked and obeyed when instructed. May every word and sentence in this book point to the One who breathes us all, with the deepest gratitude to Him who upholds us in His hands.

There are many more stories that I can share; some were in life-and-death situations, and others were in front of a group of eleven witnesses. Another involved saving a Nigerian diplomat surrounded by seven youths with a knife pointed to his neck, but something happened, and they fled. All had nothing to do with me other than I saw, heard, and responded. It is in our humanity and humility that we are strong. Only when we get out of the way and stop interfering with the Word (Rhema) can the Spirit move and blow into any situation and breathe life into it. You will find the Spirit and life-giving power whenever you have a Rhema word.

In the case of the *written* Word, however, this is different in most situations. You can know the Word, but you may not have eyes to see or ears to hear the Spirit of the written Word. As Yeshua said, "My words are Spirit and life."

Not that we are sufficient of ourselves to think of anything as being from ourselves, but our sufficiency is from God, who also made us sufficient as ministers of the new covenant, not of the letter but of the Spirit; for the letter kills, but the Spirit gives life.

- 2 Corinthians 3:5-6

Religions may claim the rights to the Word, it can be taught with full knowledge and all the fancy information and prophecies that go with the Word, but if they don't know the Spirit behind the Word, then the Word itself becomes null and void, like dead men's bones, with no marrow in it. We can all say we know something because we have heard or read about it, but only once we have experienced it can we know it. The Spirit is always hovering like a dove waiting to breathe and accompany us here so that it can be the Comforter it wants to be, but are we creating a space and a place of peace to land on?

There are many more stories that I can share, but I will leave those for now. I hope you will see and understand how this beautiful connection we call 'faith' forms and develops. Let me add this before we go further into the dimensions of the inner whispers of the small still voice. I could have easily avoided unnecessary suffering if I hadn't been so prideful, arrogant, insecure, and needing a cure. Instead, I listened to the voice of *"I know what's best for me,"* the voice of rebellion, the voice that spoke from the hardness of an overly protective heart, one that wasn't able, ready, or in a place even to want to. I was just not in a position to listen.

In the *Gospel of John 10:27*, Yeshua says:

"My sheep hear My voice, and I know them, and they follow Me."

They hear and listen because they know that his ways are always for the good of their well-being, so they follow. I was not a "sheep." I was more like a stubborn mule, full of pride and hurt and unable to hear any other voice besides my self-importance. And that's not the position to listen to the voice of God, his Word (Rhema) that could speak to all of us now. So, the real question is, do we recognise it? Can we genuinely discern its sound, its wave, its texture? This is the first and most crucial aspect of receiving and hearing the inner small, still voice. We can listen to it, but are we receiving it with an open and humble heart? We can listen to it, but do we even want to receive its wisdom?

The hearing and the listening must be ready to be followed so that **faith** becomes **actions**. And that process must come from knowledge from an encounter, a real living experience. And once the meeting has been experienced, its loving hands felt, its everlasting compassion allowed to reach your broken soul, then and only then will you rest in its loving hands and become like the sheep who know and recognise the voice of the good shepherd. No one can ever teach you how to hear the small still voice. They can point you to how to align your ears in a better, more conducive way to listen so you can recognise it for yourself, but no more than that. This is what happened to Samuel the Prophet. You can read about it in the Old Testament Bible (*1 Samuel 3*); when Samuel hears the voice but doesn't recognise it, even mistaking it for someone else voice, but he never recognised it as it was new to him.

We don't teach children to hear or see because that happens naturally, and what they choose to listen to eventually is what they desire in their own time and in their way. That's why I know in my own life that God was constantly speaking to me. Even when I look back at my childhood, he was always there, but only that I wasn't listening.

And as we all know, there are many voices we choose to listen to every day of our lives. Some are healthy, and others may appear to be but are deceptive. We all know there are many traps here on earth, many voices that can come sounding with all the right words but are motivated with wrong and evil intentions. We all know that people can talk with their lips but inwardly mean other things. And all these voices are described as false teachers, false gurus with false promises that come in many disguises, in sheep's clothing but inside are like wolves. And unfortunately, it is creeping into every part of our society and from every channel and direction. This is only half of the battle because there are two sounds we need to tackle, and when I mean tackle, I mean silencing the outer sounds filled with their distractions and selfish motives, looking to make more profit. And then there are the inner sounds we face daily, which are far more deceptive and dangerous. Far more hazardous because they are closer to us. They live and have their home in us, and if we don't know how to silence them, we end up naively feeding them until they utterly consume, oppress, depress and suppress our lives. These internal toxins can destroy us with fear, anxiety, and an overly worried mind to the point that we cannot enjoy the sweetness of stillness. And when this happens, it becomes increasingly difficult to access the inner voice, not because God is unwilling but because other sounds and feelings disconnect us. I know, and am sure you know, people that even when the sun is shining brightly, the birds are singing, and the flowers are blooming, find reasons to complain as though they are living in another reality, missing the beauty of the moment. No matter how much you try to convince them of how beautiful life can be, they just cannot and won't connect with it. The same sun that is reaching out to me is reaching them. It's unfortunate when this happens, but it happens.

Be still and know that I am God.

- Psalm 46:10

Another text speaks of "split the rock," the rock of hardness in me when I had hardened my heart towards the gentle, still, loving whisper of truth and felt I couldn't trust anyone anymore. I had listened to people that were close and tricked repeatedly, and so I, the ego-self, had agreed with myself, *"From now on, I will do it myself through hard work and fight my way through."* I had humbled myself to all the wrong voices except the inner voice of Love and Truth. And one day, I was walking alone near a park I had visited and heard the inner voice in the past and was contemplating the feeling and questioning why I had hardened my heart.

When I turned to the Logos in Matthew chapter 17, when Yeshua transfigured, taking Peter, James, and John with him on a mountain, and suddenly Moses, *(representing the Law)*, and Elijah, the prophets turned up. A voice from a cloud appeared and said, "This is my son, whom I love; with him, I am well pleased. Listen to him!" When I read **"Listen to him"**, suddenly it was as though Spirit and life filled my entire being. "Listen to him, and stop listening to the noise of your past, all the false prophets, and the people in your life who have no interest in you. Listen to Him and let His voice guide your steps, listen to Him because His Word is pure, undefiled, without any trace of ego. Steven, my son, listen to Him, for He deeply cares for you. Listen to His report only, for His Word is my Word, and his actions are a true reflection of mine, listen to him and let his Word fill your life with loving kindness."

I know the Logos as the power that turns towards contemplation and requires humility to silence the outer voices of distraction and the Rhema as the internal voice that silences the other voices and, in between, is **stillness**. When this threefold cord is applied: Logos, Rhema and Stillness, we are filled with the presence of His love.

The Hebrew word for whisper is *Demamah*, the feminine noun for (silent) whisper, and they are used together like a whisper and a voice, like in *Psalm 107:29*:

He settleth the storm into a whisper.

The storms in our lives settle by the truth and whispers of the Rhema and the Logos that silence our outer and inner worlds filled with all its distractions and noise. "Peace. Be still" is a command that Yeshua uses to calm the Sea of Galilee when his students fear losing their lives during a storm.

Then He arose and rebuked the wind and said to the sea, "Peace, be still!"

And the wind ceased, and there was a great calm.

- Gospel of Mark 4:39

With a calm assurance, he stilled the raging waters, muzzled the seas' mouth, and with a gentle whisper, the elements had to settle. And we, too, must calm down and surrender to the Word that is full of peace and never returns void but always establishes what it intends to do because when He speaks, everything has to move in our lives and align with it. And this experience can be for every soul that seek Truth. Truth has unlimited channels from which to express itself. Truth is everywhere if we know where and how to look, but we must be ready to hear it, listen and then to follow it.

Peace - trust, settle, let go, stop gripping, stop fighting, put the sword down, end the fight, lay your weapons down, drop the walls you placed around your heart, afraid to come out and be who you are: peace, my brother and my sister. Peace.

Be - be, return to being, for you are being. In other words, you are alive because it is breathing you. You are, not because you did the work, so please let go and enter into your true home of Being, existing as an expression of, as an overflow of the same mind and thoughts of The All. So be and allow this word to melt your heart.

Stillness - your place of refuge, where you will hear its quiet, gentle voice and come to know your true essence, where you can grow and form as it was meant. The meeting place where Spirit and life can merge with you, where even the word communion melts, and the peace that surpasses all logic and all understanding is felt in every cell, every part and particle of our being. *Stillness* is the condition, alignment, quality, and space, the sacred substance we call peace; the atmosphere where all our noise slowly melts away and our true light comes to the surface. In this peaceful, clean, pure condition, the living word of Truth, both within and without, wants to manifest in our lives. And always remember what I have said – don't just take what I am saying as Truth. Instead, examine and test it for yourself with genuine humility.

Listen to Truth - if you don't know where to look, then look at Yeshua – listen to his words, for they are Spirit and life, Logos and Rhema, for your internal and external life. Let these two forces meet in the privacy of your room, where only God sees and will reward you.

But you, when you pray, go into your room, and when you have shut your door, pray to your Father who is in the secret place; and your Father who sees in secret will reward you openly.

- Gospel of Matthew 6:6

Let His peace silence the outer distractions and the internal toxins. Open the space and sit in stillness, and stillness, by its pure eternal residing untarnished nature, free of all pollutions, will attract the Logos and the Rhema. But only if you are ready to sit and listen. And I mean **listen**, not just hear. To listen is to follow, even if it means facing everything you have avoided, running away from, and being afraid to confront. So be prepared to be challenged, shaken, uprooted, amazed, and left with peace.

The next chapter will explore the unlimited ways and channels the Word and Way of Truth can communicate. But there is one condition: that you put aside all religious dogmas and dead and damaging beliefs. The light of Truth can appear to us in any form as The All is formless. He can materialise at any moment, for he is beyond time. Light and Truth have no artificial restrictions set by rigid, stale beliefs. So please cast aside all dogmas that restrict you in any way from the dawn of Truth reaching out to you. Please don't wait for a time when you are in a desperate condition, holding on to dear life, or when you have come to the end of your life are like one of the criminals on the side of Yeshua on the cross, pleading to be saved. We don't need to wait or suffer more than we already have.

CONTEMPLATION & REFLECTION

Has anything hardened your heart?

Find a warm, comfortable place to sit, as you deserve. Your Spirit deserves the warm, gentle embrace of this moment. It deserves to settle into the stillness of this moment and, more importantly so that the warmth of God's loving truth can sink deeply into your heart.

You are becoming aware of your sacred breath, inhaling and exhaling. Can you feel the ocean, the waves moving in your in and out breath? Allow the breath that is breathing you to calm your mind naturally. And ask yourself these questions.

Have I become hardened to receive the truth?

Is there anything I resist because I am afraid to visit and face the consequences?

Have I placed safety walls around it in case I get hurt again?

What changes am I afraid to face?

Have I boxed my life into false ideas and concepts that I am gripping and preventing the truth from reaching me?

Please give your heart the time and space to ask these questions.

You will know the truth, and the truth will set you free.
- Gospel of John 8:32

CHAPTER 6

SPIRIT, LIGHT AND PRESENCE

As we move into **Spirit**, **Light** and **Presence**, I would like to add that if we are walking in Truth, then Truth will keep reminding us of what we need to hear, even if we are begging on our hands and knees to receive something else. So, the previous chapters would be keys before getting to this point in our journey. To live and act by faith requires real listening because when we receive truth, we first need to allow that to penetrate every fibre of our being, and then faith can grow. Without real listening, we cannot hear the voice of Truth when it speaks to us, so how can you expect to hear the small still voice if you can't even listen when it speaks? Allow me to explain; if you have a friend that you love and care about, and they had an issue in their life that you recognised was damaging them and was affecting their health or relationships, if they approached you for a chat, would you tell them despite knowing that they might get offended or even defensive? If you loved and cared for them, you would point it out so they would stop causing further damage, right?

What would you say if they got offended and left and then, after three years, returned in a worse condition and with the same damaging habits? Would you discuss and reveal the mysteries of the Universe with them, or would you first lovingly reach out and try to help them? The second, of course, is what happens with the Truth. It shines its light through its breath, *Spirit*, not because it wants to make you feel bad, ashamed, or fearful, but the complete opposite. It is so that you can enjoy a new liberty and walk with a fresh lightness in your steps. It never points the finger but always shines its light, and the nature of light is to reveal, not to expose. We do that to each other when we gossip and tare people down, exposing them. So please don't mistake the ways of the Eternal light-giving, life-saving, all-loving Presence of the One.

The light shines, all is revealed, and the things that surface first require cleaning. That's the very nature of a Presence that is both holy and whole. It can feel uncomfortable when the light of Truth shines and reveals the mess. But it doesn't have to be if you know that the Presence is loving, calling you back. If you only knew that you could run to it with all your mess, all the garbage, and all the wasteful stuff that has cluttered your life. This sweet Presence whispering to you, *"Come to me, all who are heavily laden, cast your burdens unto me, for I care for you deeply. I always have and always will. Give me your burden, and I will take care of your load. You can't do it yourself; that's why I came"*.

There is never any condemnation when we turn our hearts and draw close to this Presence. It is loving-kindness and wants to cover, clean and merge with us. It is full of truth that wants to awaken our minds and reveal everything that separates us from the love of God, and I mean **everything**. It all has to go because He is whole and wants a complete union.

I cannot force or teach anyone to hear or feel this Presence, but I can point out when it is a sacred Presence because I have come to know it. I have heard its voice and seen its face. I have felt its embrace in every cell of my being and filled my heart with a most intense love for all my brothers and sisters, every creature, every tree, all of creation, and every sentient being. And I know it will do the same for you. In this, I am certain because there is only one Source, one Light, one Spirit, and one Presence. The Presence is not what man-made religions have turned it into. This Presence never points to your past like some wicked taskmaster wrapping you deeper into feelings of guilt from mistakes that we have all made. This is not the Presence of God's light and love. Instead, it wants to forgive and mend you from all the wrong you may have done, every act, big or small, things that you have done in public and private, the things that are weighing you down. He wants this because He loves every fibre of you. Every part of your life means everything to the One who created you from His heart. You were birthed from His Presence and the centre of its loving overflow. His heart grieves when we are out of sync or in disharmony. I know this because I experienced it.

I have searched and searched, and with all my failings, with all my weaknesses and with all my mistakes, but when I came face to face with this loving Presence, it was all Love, a Love immersed with the nature and substance of Peace, and immense blazing fire of Truth. I felt the covering of His Spirit and watched the mountains of my fears melt like wax close to a burning flame. Have you forgotten what happened 2000 years ago when a criminal was hanging next to the Way, the Truth and the Life, punished for his crimes and with nowhere to go? Two souls condemned to death by the punishment of crucifixion, both guilty of their crimes, yet one being remorseful and accepting the responsibility for his life *(and the penalty of his crime)* while the other remained bitter, twisted and angry. Both were crucified between Yeshua, who was condemned to die, accused of being blasphemous and all lies were made against him. Yet, this was God's plan to save the world, humanity, and sentient beings – past, present and future.

One of the criminals who hung there hurled insults at him:

"Aren't you the Messiah? Save yourself and us!" But the other

criminal rebuked him. "Don't you fear God," he said, "since you are under the same sentence? We are punished justly, for we are getting what our deeds deserve. But this man has done nothing wrong." Then he said, "Yeshua, remember me when you come into your kingdom." Yeshua answered, "Truly I tell you, today you will be with me in paradise."

- Gospel of Luke 23:39-43

There are two criminals here hanging on either side. But at the centre was Love, waiting to hear the whisper of humility, waiting for this tiny entrance of space so that He could respond with a whispered love, charged with the same power and authority to wash this criminal clean that will allow him to enter the same space that a loving Father-Mother would always want for their children, to be close to them, watch over them, protect them, and enjoy their company.

I am not focusing here on the different responses of these two criminals but instead on the presence of *Love in action*. Not when it is resting in a quiet, comfortable space, but instead, when it is hanging, gasping for every breath, stripped naked, beaten with open wounds and nailed on his hands and feet to the wooden beam. Even then, He will reach out to the most hardened criminals. Let's not mistake our love for the love of God. This type of love is not determined or quenched by the things of this world. It is not moved by emotion when it feels to. This Presence is whole, and it is complete. It moves unchanged, consistently and from its central essence, not from the thoughts under the bondage and constant reaction of duality. It is Love - therefore, it is loving. It is Truth – therefore, it speaks only truth. It is loving kindness - therefore, it reaches out to all who humble themselves and calls out, even in their final breath. It is from this Presence that the inner whispers and secrets are spoken. And this One is calling you back to return to your first love.

Return to your first love because you were born from its first love, created from the Presence and fragrance of its light. When He sent forth his Word, the light was the first visible thing; in that light was the essence of all life, every living creature. That light is the most central part of our DNA, signature and memory. Only we have forgotten it, and we have lost this memory chasing all the wrong things here in this material world, searching for it everywhere, trying our very best to fill and discover a replacement - running to and fro, like hungry ghosts from one fix to the next. It's a spiritual hole, a spiritual vacuum, a hole in the bucket of our lives that can only be filled once we turn to the most central point with genuine humility as bare and as vulnerable as the criminal pleading for mercy.

This loving Presence wants to be part of every aspect of your life, walking alongside your side as your Helper and Comforter in the garden of your life. It wants you to know that every step of your journey here can be shared with His loving Presence, helping you make the right life-giving choices. It wants to inspire your choices, and it wants you to rest when it says "*rest*". It wants you to know that you can trust its loving hands in the most challenging times. It wants you to know that the lightness of His Truth is there to help you always see what's best for you. He wants to breathe life through His Spirit into things you thought were dead, left behind, and buried. His Spirit wants to live and transfer his life-giving energy to you in the most intimate mind-to-mind transferences. His Presence wants to cover your family and children and keep them safe, helping you see the way. But we must commit, turn our hearts, and direct our sails in the right direction to catch the wind of the Spirit.

"Better is one day in Your courts than a thousand."

\- Psalm 84 v10

One day in His Presence is so fulfilling that nothing is remotely comparable. I want you to know there is fullness of joy in his Presence. Remember when there was a time when only joy existed because nothing was weighing you down? You were happy without any external reason to be. That's what it feels when you come into contact with this Presence. I am doing my best to describe this Presence to you because I want you to know it's waiting for you, and I don't want you wasting time chasing all the wrong things and looking in all the wrong places. His Presence is like bathing in a bath of eternal rest, a rest that removes all tension the moment you bathe in it. It's a rest that I can only best describe as floating with the floating Earth. Nothing seems heavy, as though you are resting in the palm of His hand. Remember, it's formless and thus able to fit into any space; it's shapeless, therefore able to enter any space. It's refreshing, unlike any water you will ever taste. Your thirst is immediately quenched when you are in the company of this Presence.

But the Helper, the Holy Spirit, whom the Father will send in my name,

will teach you all things and bring all that I have said to you to your remembrance.

\- Gospel of John 14:26

His Presence will teach you all you need to know in your daily 24-hour cycle, and you don't have to run around from one place to the next. He will become your Helper, Comforter and Teacher if you allow it. His manifestations are as limitless as every cell and particle with life in the entire Universe. There are no limits to His Presence. I could go on and on and never run out of descriptions. This calling starts with humility. This sacred call begins with your first step into the space of humility, and then allow yourself to be pulled and moved by His beautiful Spirit.

I hope that these pages have moved you a little to seek His Presence, enquire and seek for yourself until you find. Those who seek with a humble heart will soon discover and see. In the following pages, we will look at the main channels of communication that this majestic Presence uses to reach souls. And you may be shocked to discover, or maybe not, that none of them has anything to do with religion. That's way too boring for Spirit, Light, and Presence.

"Everyone who drinks this water will be thirsty again (referring to water from a well),

but whoever drinks the water I give him will never be thirsty again. The water that

I will give him will become in him a spring of water welling up to eternal life."

- Gospel of John 4:13-14

THE UNLIMITED CHANNELS OF TRUTH

When I look at your heavens, the work of your fingers, the moon and the stars

that you have established, what are human's beings that you are mindful of

them, mortals, that you care for them.

- Psalm 8:3-4

Many believe that the small, still whisper of God's eternal Holy Spirit is limited by a few channels in which He communicates to us. They restrict God like a TV box with a few channels to transfer and communicate his Eternal Truths when His Truths, if you are open, are **everywhere**. Unfortunately, once again, religions have painted the Eternal Creator of the entire complex Universe into a dull, closed, limited image in their minds, restricting people from opening their beautiful hearts that they have been told are wicked and deceitful above all things and never to trust it. Yes, we do get lost. Yes, we do miss the mark, and yes, like sheep, we follow the crowd. But, if you raise people believing that they are dammed, lost, and have a wicked and deceitful heart from the moment they can understand, they will believe these lies. However, if souls are encouraged to open their beautiful hearts and, like the psalmist David says, to "look up to the heavens and the stars and marvel at the work of God's handicraft", chances are that souls would grow and fall in love naturally with the Creator. We are to present our children to the love and safety of Christ's hands, for the heart of God and His beautiful creation belongs to them. We must become like children and come running to the Father with a pure, soft, open heart. One that is without pride and not afraid to make mistakes, marvelling at the work of His hands and in awe of the beauty of all His creation.

"Let the little children come to me, and do not hinder them, for the kingdom of God

belongs to such as these. Truly I tell you, anyone, who will not receive the kingdom

of God as a little child will never enter it." And he took the children in his arms,

placed his hands on them and blessed them.

- Gospel of Mark 10:14-16

Let's remove all the boxes you have placed around where Truth can suddenly decide to speak to you. Let's throw away all our man-made constructs and all the fears we have placed around people of faith. No wonder people all over the world are running away from these boring, restrictive chains that your so-called religious teachers are putting around people as though you are an authority on how a creative God that's woven every dot and detail of his creation chooses to speak to his creation. How dare we interfere with that sacred space between a soul and its Creator! So, I hope when you read these following pages, your hearts will open to the beauty of who God created you to be, of the individual creative heart that only you have, and open it as wide as a child running back to the loving arms. May you find your song if you are a singer or songwriter, paint your pictures with Him and play your musical instruments, walk together in His beautiful nature, let your hair down once again, and trust that you can live in Him. He in you, fully let go in all the ways he wants to communicate to you. So, let's look at some of the ways the All; the I AM – communicates. Please be patient with me here because I will use the same text and books the religious folks have used that close these channels.

Lift your eyes high and see: who created these? He who brings out their host by number, calling them all by name, by the greatness of his might and because he is strong in power, and not one is missing.

- Isaiah 40:26

Notice the part where it says "calling them all by name"? Yes! Every star in the Universe is named, and names to God are very important as they contain and carry vital information, revelation and deep insight about who you are and your life's purpose. Hence, names are also an important communication channel. But we will go into names a little deeper later in the book. Here is another example:

Therefore, the Lord Himself will give you a sign: Behold, the virgin shall conceive and bear a Son, and shall call His name Immanuel (meaning "God with us")

- Isaiah 7:14

So, you can see that names are among the many ways the All communicates, often used to establish a new agreement or movement and sometimes used to start a new path and beginning in someone's life.

Saul, who was persecuting and killing the followers of Yeshua (Christ), became Paul when he encountered the risen Christ during one of his travels, and a new path was paved for him. The very name Yeshua means "God saves", revealing his purpose and calling. In the *Gospel of Matthew chapter 2*, Matthew uses the Greek word "Magi" to describe those who came to pay homage to Yeshua upon his arrival to Earth. The term likely refers to experts in astrology. Men had given their lives to studying the movement of the stars, and that was how they knew the arrival of the promised Messiah/Saviour would come to Earth.

Genesis 1:14 says the stars, along with the sun and moon, were given for signs and seasons - meaning they had a message to mark time and seasons, but like the Magi, stars could also reveal the birth of someone that would change the course and direction of humanity.

When Buddha was asked his name, he replied, "I am awakened", translated as "the Buddha" (also meaning "enlightened one, a knower". These names give us an indication of our Creator's intention for their lives here on Earth.

NAMES, STARS and CREATION are just three channels through which we can know God communicates. They will be powerless if these channels are taken out of context, out of their correct alignment, and taken for selfish gain without surrendering to the Truth. An example of this is in the life of Daniel *(chapter 2)* – the Astrologers of the Babylonian court were powerless in interpreting the King's dream. Yet, Daniel was the one who was able to interpret. This shows that, despite knowing text or the readings of the stars, it will amount to nothing unless it is God-breathed. Just knowing things do not determine whether God is speaking to you. This is the same with the Magi who visited the birth of Yeshua – they didn't have the text to know the exact location of the Messiah's birth, so when they visited Herod to enquire about these details, the scribes and the religious leaders, although having the text, did not even set foot to go and seek the long-awaited Messiah, but only giving the information to the Magi:

"But you, Bethlehem Ephrathah,

Though you are little among the thousands of Judah,

Yet out of you shall come forth to Me

The One to be Ruler in Israel,

Whose goings forth are from of old,

From everlasting."

– Micah 5:2

Even when the scribes opened their books, knowing the prophecy by the Prophet Micah, they still could not see, perhaps because they were not open to seeing. And if you are not open to seeing, you will remain in that condition.

Sacred texts are also a beautiful and powerful way that God speaks. However, for the text to speak into your life, you cannot just merely read it. It has to be read through you, not the other way around. If your life is not aligned with the text or is unwilling to align with it, how can you expect God's blessings and promises to manifest in your life? The condition is you have to be **open** to receiving the Truth, not from your interpretation, but through the living Spirit who can interpret and translate the text and become a mirror to your life. Reading, studying and doing have to go hand in hand. This is *faith in action*. So, now we have NAMES, STARS, CREATION, and TEXT as means of The All communicating with us.

Be still, and know that I am God

– Psalm 46:10

I have mentioned stillness before, *"Be still and know"* - In stillness, prayer becomes a dialogue and not a monologue. Prayer with deep stillness is one of the most powerful ways to hear the text. Notice I said to hear the text and not read the text. In stillness, you hear the sound of the sound, the secret word (Rhema) speaking to you. In stillness, you hear the inner whispers. The inner whisper of the text and the inner whisper within are similar in their transference and feeling when receiving them.

Animals can also be a means of communication if you are open and the moment is right. For example, when a donkey speaks to Balaam, you can read the story in *Numbers 22:22 (Old Testament)*. But these are unusual; it was Balaam's donkey and part of his 24-hour cycle, and if you are working closely with animals, it might be one of the ways.

In 2019, I encountered a bird that fell on my path after having a dream of it. I was prompted to pray for it by the Spirit, and afterwards, it recovered, leaving me with a message that changed my life forever.

Then there are messengers both from the Heavens and the Earth who carry specific messages. I have personally encountered both, but the following texts testify to that:

For he will command his angels concerning you to guard you in all your ways.
On their hands, they will bear you up lest you strike your foot against a stone.

- Psalm 91:11-12

My God sent his angel and shut the lions' mouths, and they have not harmed me
because I was found blameless before him; and also before you,
O King, I have done no harm.

- Daniel 6:22

See that you do not despise one of these little ones. For I tell you that in
heaven, their angels always see the face of my Father who is in heaven.

- Gospel of Matthew 18:10

"Or do you think that I cannot now pray to My Father, and
He will provide Me with more than twelve legions of angels?

- Gospel of Matthew 26:53

There are channels in our 24-hour cycles like music, film, song, theatre, books we read, friends we have, circumstances, or cycles of history that suddenly speak to you. It can happen to while having coffee with a friend who suddenly says something that hits a cord in your heart. Even circumstances or numbers that appear will carry a sign and message for you. My point is: God is not bound by anything. As long as we are in place and positioned to receive with an open and humble heart, anything is possible. A life of prayer, meditation in the quiet, a fresh breeze of His Presence is the place I would point every soul to, and with the text for contemplation. However, not every soul likes this, and that is perfectly fine. Also, God knows us, so if you find reading text and praying mundane, and prefer dancing with a joyful heart, then do that wholeheartedly.

And David danced before the Lord with all his might.

- 2 Samuel 6:14

So, if it's dance, do it wholeheartedly as though it's your last dance. If it's quiet reading, meditation and reflection, again, do it wholeheartedly and not as a tedious ritual you have to do. Be honest, and the One who planted that expression of authentic true honesty in you will be moved. David was declared as a man after God's own heart (*Book of Acts 13:22*)

I often go for long walks and dance to music in my local forest, then sit absorbed by the beauty of God's creation and my goodness me, this is the most enjoyable. It is all beauty, and everything will speak of God's loving kindness. When the soul has surrendered, they become still, and the unmistakable voice of God appears everywhere, exposing all the fake voices and distractions. The clear translation of God appears, and you will experience his living waters inside and outside you.

So, keep one whole day for yourself and The All; keep it your sacred day. This once-a-week meeting with your Maker, away from work and all the usual things you do on a day-to-day basis, a day where you can totally switch off (including your phone) and turn your heart upwards in a mode of prayer, meditate, read the text, contemplate, talk to God from your deepest honesty, and see what happens. This is your Sabbath day - a day of rest.

Essentially, we all need channels to be open to hearing the sacred whispers of the Sacred One daily. The benefits are too many to write about, so get your diary, take notes, and observe what happens to your life. You owe it to yourself and The All.

YOU ALWAYS MATTERED

In this next portion of the book, I want to reveal some honest, heartfelt whispers that you may not have had the opportunity to hear. Unfortunately, many of us who grow up in this increasingly competitive material world are forced to overwork and compete to survive. With inflation and the rising cost of living, people are being forced into tough situations and left with little or no time to focus on things that really matter. Parents often have to work two jobs, leaving their children waiting and yearning for their attention, appreciation, and loving affection.

We all know that the material world is a destructive rat race, where the "dog eats dog" mentality prevails. I have nothing against all of us working together lovingly, as long as the systems and structures we work will benefit everyone—from the smallest creatures to the greatest, to the air we breathe, the poor and needy, the streams and oceans we share, marine life, and all other sentient beings.

But the way the world is spinning, suicide rates, depression, anxiety, and mental health issues have skyrocketed worldwide, making people feel unwanted, tired, broken, confused, and frustrated. Apart from the rich to the super-rich, people from all walks of life have all felt the increasing demands globally. Some are changing professions and moving into other sectors because of the ever-increasing downward spiral that most feel they cannot fix.
As a result, many souls are lost further in feeling unwanted, unloved, used, or abused. These types of suffering have longer-lasting effects, and some people have even tried to commit suicide because they were beginning to feel there was no point in living, feeling hopeless and completely dejected.

You may be experiencing hopelessness right now, or perhaps you know someone who is. This message is for you, and for your precious heart. You may not have realized just how wanted and needed you are, or how sacred and loved you are, even before you took shape or form and were incarnated on Planet Earth.

I want to remind you of a point and a place that is recorded in your very DNA, at your very sacred centre, where you matter, and where the very nature of Love deeply loves you—a love bursting for you to return to this hidden memory waiting to be rediscovered.

Sometimes memories are forgotten, and the longer we are away from this point, the further away from it we go.

The place and point I am referring to is your most authentic memory, beyond all the memories you have imprinted and forgotten. It is a memory that, when aroused and awoken within you, will lead you to the place where all your past destructive memories begin to make sense.

In this sacred memory, imprinted in your deepest parts, lies the cause of why you have felt alone, searching for meaning and connection. Even amidst all the madness, a gentle and loving hand wants to walk with you and whisper secrets and wisdom into your being. It wants to breathe its love and remind you of how special, sacred, and loved you are, telling you that you have always mattered. But you have forgotten it; it is buried inside. Now, it is time for you to reawaken it!

When we were children, playing with our friends away from the dramas that adults always seem to be involved in, there was always a place in our hearts where we felt a connection, a union, and a deep sense of timelessness. We could play for long hours without getting tired, even if it was only with stones or glass marbles. There was an invisible connection with everything and everyone. We may not have been able to express it intellectually, but as children, we felt it. We never questioned it and were happy to just be. There was a lightness everywhere, and life and humans lived from it. It was not gained in churches or through religious rituals. It was just a force within and without, naturally there without any effort.

This presence was living, and we did not interfere with it. It was there dancing with the birds, moving within the trees, twinkling through the stars at night, but no one ever talked about it. I could see it and feel it everywhere. The dance of the light was all around, shining its light, yet most of us miss it as we grow older. Yeshua himself quoted it from the text:

> But when the chief priests and scribes saw the wonderful things that He did, and the children crying out in the temple and saying, "Hosanna to the Son of David!" they were indignant and said to Him, "Do You hear what these are saying?" And Jesus said to them, "Yes. Have you never read,

'Out of the mouth of babes and nursing infants

You have perfected praise'?"

- Gospel of Matthew 21:15-16

Yeshua was quoting from the Old Testament's *Psalm of David chapter 8 verse 22*, so let's look at this text deeper and let me ask you a question: How can they have *"**perfected praise**"* unless it was already there? A baby's response is the most natural; it is pure, untarnished, without dogma or religious indoctrination, education or schooling. It is essentially one, inseparable from the Source, totally and completely being breathed, with no effort or trying. They just are.

"Let the little children come to me, and do not hinder them, for the

kingdom of God belongs to such as these." (Yeshua speaking)

- Gospel of Matthew 19:14

Suppose we allow our children and the next generation to grow in their most natural and original state, abiding and remaining in oneness. In that case, we have to give them space to grow naturally, trusting that they are already in perfect alignment. We must allow them to mature at their own pace and time, without hindering or imposing any expectations on them based on our selfish desires. We should not try to mold them in our image because they are already much closer to God's authentic image and likeness than we are.

Think about it: when we are in the company of nursing infants, our hearts naturally melt and soften. It's because of their innocence and purity, and purity is the source. They are more **spirit** than flesh, untarnished and untainted by the scars of pain, suffering, dogmas, or indoctrination.

Let me encourage you with this: deep within you, beyond the noise, muck, and hardness of the past, lies a fountain of perfect love and a river of joy that is blissful and full of peace. This river carries the memory of your true ancient past.

Just as He chose us in Him before the foundation of the world,

that we should be holy and without blame before Him in love.

- Ephesians 1:4

We were at the forefront of God's intentions, the heartbeat and pulse of His thoughts. When He said, "**let there be light**," we were there in that light; our lives, our spirits, our character, our entire beings came into existence in that moment. Although we may not remember it yet, we can certainly begin the journey of rediscovering it. It is closer than our very breath and the reason for our breath; it's the Breath that breathes us. This light is who we are beyond all hindrances we have experienced; beyond all pain, suffering, fears, and doubts, lies the eternal memory of our Maker's loving imprints. We are His Mind, and He is buried in us, waiting to be reawakened. It's our first love, our perfected song, the untarnished fearless expression of this light. Let us renew this love and allow it to overflow in every cell. Oh, awaken in us!

If we observe the lives of Yeshua and Buddha, we will realize that they lived from a pure place - one soul had to discover it, while the other never left it. However, both pointed to the same point of existence. Therefore, there is no need to search elsewhere. When the All said, "let there be light," He also proclaimed that we are already perfect.

"Therefore, you shall be perfect, just as your father in heaven is perfect."

- Gospel of Matthew 5:48

In other words, the pure light of perfection has brought you into existence out of this perfection, and therefore, you are the result. This is fantastic news! All the running around chasing our tails is unnecessary when we realize that we are perfect, whole, and complete just as we are. Allowing ourselves to be who we are does not interfere with God's comprehensive and excellent work. We do not try to change the trees, streams, sun, and moon because doing so would cause a hugely destructive problem. The same applies to us. We cannot do this ourselves because it is not our work. There is no need to doubt yourself anymore. You do not doubt trees, grass, or ants, so there is no need to doubt yourself. Open your hearts and allow this truth to remind you that you are the light of the world, and light requires no additions. You should never feel alone, worthless, abandoned, or without a purpose because you came from the same light that created the universe, the one that we all marvel at. Now, it is time to marvel at you! You are a marvel, a wonder, and you have always mattered! The Living Bible version of *Ephesians 1:4-6* is wonderful:

"Long ago, before he made the world, God chose us to be his very own."

So, you see, we don't belong in this increasingly demanding world. We are not slaves to this world. We belong to the loving hands of a God who breathed His very essence into us. We belong to Him, and only when we realize this will the void in our hearts ever be filled. We are His. So, if you are hearing this for the first time today, you can gently begin to quietly and privately ask God yourself to prove this. Ask Him yourself. Don't believe me, or because it's written in the text. Ask like a child who truly wants to know, even if it means that everything you have learned has distorted the truth. We all have to eat humble pie sometimes.

Before I formed you in the womb, I knew and approved you;

before you were born, I set you apart.

- Jeremiah 1:5

Every soul is crafted with a completely different flavour, a unique and intricate expression of God's creation, intimately known by the Creator who names every star and blade of grass. Every part of you has been carefully thought out and set apart for a specific purpose that only you can fulfil. In the heart and mind of God, a very sacred and unique purpose is reserved for you. That's why you don't need to fight for your place or get defensive or compete with anyone else, because only you can fulfil that purpose. This also applies to married couples, who are brought together by cords of love arranged by the Perfect Mind, not the mind of tradition.

I may be the least gifted soul, but I know that God has a small part for me that only I can fulfil, and no one can take that away from me. Even if others try to hate me for it, it's only because they haven't yet discovered their own purpose. So instead of boasting like Joseph did to his brothers, causing pain and jealousy, I will privately point to it with the loving fruits of my life. This is the way.

God's kingdom is different from man-made kingdoms, which are always wrestling and competing with one another. In His domain, all we have to do is trust His hand and learn to walk in His timing, without striving or pushing. It may sound simple, but it's true, and Yeshua gave His life so that we could realize this. Each of our lives has a unique tune, a song that only we can sing at our turn and reignite our love union with God. The Holy Breath of God will once again breathe through our lives, and we will feel like children, yet with a mind that can comprehend and articulate the connection. All we need to do is flow with its harmony and life, dancing together and writing new songs, and together we will write new pages in our book.

You were formed with great detail in your mother's womb, by the One who sees every one of the trillion cells that make you and has designed every part of your life with a unique expression. You are carrying this memory within you. Can you feel your majestic uniqueness yet? You were mindfully woven and knit together in that way, and everything around you supports your life here on Earth.

I will praise You, for I am fearfully *and* wonderfully made;

Marvellous are Your works, and *that* my soul knows very well.

- Psalm 139:14

You were created to shine as the stars do and give life as the sun does, so extend your creative branches and paint your picture. You carry the work of a Creator who was mindful of you before you were ever born, and with His creative Mind, He breathed you in wonder, amazement, and awe. When you finally sit and rest in these eternal truths, you will know the love that existed before and ultimately rest in Yeshua's last prayer and wishes for all of us, when He said:

"That the love with which you loved Me may be in them, and I in them"

- Gospel of John 17:26

The love He is talking about started when He said, *'Let there be light.'* And there you were, intimately, skilfully woven and thought about. You were created to live a life that reflects this light - a life that is one with the Light, in the way you have been set apart for and uniquely chosen. So step into your rightful place, where the 'reserved seat' has your name on it.

Be still and know that I am God

- Psalm 46:10

BE STILL - the only thing we must be. In stillness, God reveals Himself. It happens in His sacred presence, for you are His first love. So let us return to His call together and allow our hearts to awaken and reawaken to His eternal love.

YOUR TRUE CROWN

Do you know that you have a beautiful crown? One that only fits your beautiful mind, a crown that perfectly fits the shape of your skull, designed and shaped with you in mind? It is a crown that is fit for you only, specifically designed for the way you think, the way you want to create, the way you want to inspire others, the way you want to write, for the jokes you want to laugh at and share, for the wisdom you want to manifest. And this crown is a sign and symbol that you, my dear brother and sister, are set apart for a unique and particular task, a calling that only you can fulfil. It's a crown that speaks of your role in this life. So, you have a crown, and I want you to place it on your head if you have placed it down because, as I said before, YOU MATTER.

Your life matters. Your speech, your thoughts matter to God and All That Is. Your life matters to the ants, the birds of the air, the forest you walk in, and to me and all living creatures. You count, so please hear the voice calling you to place the crown back on your head, for it is your light and glory. It matters because, like everything in the entire universe that has a rank, position, alignment, and place, and so do you. I know others have tried to tear down your crown at times, making you feel you don't fit here or have a role. But it's a lie, and I want you to listen to me for just a second. Those who have caused you to place your crown down or have tried to shame you or cause you harm only do such things because they haven't realized their own crowns. They haven't realized their own positions, so they have been after yours. Please pick up your crown and place it back on your head. This crown is your gift and cannot be taken away from you unless you, yourself, remove it.

Behold, I am coming quickly! Hold fast what you have,

that no one may take your crown.

- Revelation 3:11

When we stop standing up in life and let our true colours shine, we rob ourselves of the very life designed for us. Similarly, when we stop others because they don't quite look the part, sound different, or think differently and have different views, we take their crowns off. Unless humanity understands this universal law, it will seek to create robots, and there will always be rebellion. Rebellious energy can damage the soul manifesting it and all those around it.

This crown also speaks of the blessing of your character that has been tried and tested over time and seasons. It declares what a wonderful mother or father you have been, what a great friend you have been, and all the kind acts you have done. It speaks of the time spent alone working and making a living to provide for your beloved family and friends. It is your crown, so please don't take it off anymore. Wear it with humility always but never take it off. It is the crown of your precious and sacred life.

Blessed is the one who perseveres under trial because, having stood the test,

That person will receive the crown of life that the Lord has promised to

those who love him.

- James 1:12

This crown is for those who love and continue to love even when the world urges them to seek revenge. It's for those who dare to bless others even when it's easier to curse them. This crown is imbued with the sweat, blood, and tears of those who persevere. I'm not referring to the labor of selfish sacrifices for personal gain and power. James' text didn't refer to that kind of crown either. The crown I'm referring to is one that has already been placed upon you. It beckons you to lay down your life for a friend. This crown is for those who have touched the earth with their heads because they want to love, forgive, and walk the path of selflessness in a world that constantly encourages us to live for ourselves rather than for our destined crown. The crown created for you must be merged with the One who created it. It's a crown that has been placed on your head by a Maker who knows every hair on your head. So receive it and let Him place it on you. It belongs to you, and your name is written on it. If you walk in your calling and finish your race, this crown has the potential to bear twelve precious stones. Sadly, some wear the crown for self-glorification, living only to please their egos. In doing so, they develop the wrong kind of stones. Such people seek to rule and dominate with an iron rod to satisfy themselves. However, this is not the crown that has been prepared for you. The one that is encouraged to be pursued, developed, and brought into the material world.

The crown that I'm referring to is not of this world but from another dimension, and it can only be worn in all its glory if the soul is willing to walk the narrow path that leads to life. For what does it profit a person to gain the whole world yet lose their soul? Whoever desires to wear this crown must first lay aside their own selfish desires and ambitions. This crown has been prepared for you by a pure mind, far beyond anything that can be worked out with intellect, reason, or logic. It's a crown that has been measured for you by the most refined of minds, the one that sees your life from a vast perspective. It comes from the mind that knows the best way for you to live. Before I talk about your crown's twelve potential precious stones, I want to remind you of the crown that Yeshua wore. Observing his crown, we will better understand our own crown.

When they had twisted a crown of thorns, they put it on His head, and a reed in His right hand. And they bowed the knee before Him and mocked Him, saying, "Hail, King of the Jews!" Then they spat on Him, and took the reed and struck Him on the head. And when they had mocked Him, they took the robe off Him, put His own clothes on Him, and led Him away to be crucified.

- Gospel of Matthew 27:29-31

If you know roses with the sweetest fragrance, you will also know that thorns protect them. These thorns are like sharp knives protecting them from both humans and animals. This is the first thing you need to know about the loving sacrifice that wore the Crown of Thorns upon himself so that through the **Mind of Christ** (our true crown), the fragrance of sacrificial love in our hearts may be protected. Some scholars interpret this as him taking every curse of our minds upon himself, but I see it differently. I see thorns as something that can separate us from the heart and centre of God's love. I see the thorns as everything in our lives that separates us from His eternal sweet-smelling fragrance of unconditional love.

"You will know them by their fruits.
Do men gather grapes from thornbushes or figs from thistles?"

- Gospel of Matthew 7:16

The absence of God's sweet-smelling fragrance in our lives leaves us in a very similar condition to that of thorns - stiff, defensive, prickly, and cutting. I see the Crown of Thorns as a constant reminder of every act, process, and manifestation of all the actions that lead us away from the very heart of The All, the rose. When we take loving-kindness away from our schools, families, relationships, and communities, they soon become defensive and distant from the heart of the matter, losing its warm, embracing, sweet, gentle fragrance.

Instead, stiff, prickly pride replaces its position, and soon sharp knives and words fly everywhere. Yeshua took those thorns upon himself so that we could return to the all-loving union that God wants to have with all His creation.

We were not created to live like thorns, far from the centre of God's heart's rose, being stiff-necked, cutting down one another and causing harm. We were intended to be a sweet-smelling fragrance of God's love. It's loving-kindness that carries the Crown of Glory, and it was loving-kindness that wore the Crown of Thorns to the cross. There is no greater crown than laying your life down for all sentient beings. This is the fragrance that has to carry all our crowns. And when we put on this Mind, our hearts and minds are protected by the sweet-smelling aroma of His love and light.

Even though the Crown of Thorns was meant as a mockery, humiliation, and shame, Love was still watching, reflecting, and transferring the fragrance, unmoved with unconditional love currents and streams of the highest vibrations. In that atmosphere, those very cursed thorns became the biggest blessing for those who had eyes to see and ears to hear. The power in the Crown of Thorns was worn for you and me so that we could be the jewels on His Crown and His Love in ours, carrying the fragrance of a close and intimate friendship.

What was made a mockery became life-giving. Can you see the power in this Crown of Thorns? Can you see that even in your own life, when you feel a million miles away, like Yeshua when surrounded by blood-thirsty wicked hearts, God's love does not change? It doesn't matter what circumstance you may find yourself in, who is mocking, teasing, and spitting lies about you or trying to humiliate you. What matters is whether or not you are wearing the crown of God's love - the love that changes not, the steadfast love that never ceases. That is the real question: to love or not to love?

Someone once asked me, "If there was no New Testament, how would you know Yeshua died on the cross?" I replied, "Simple, there was no New Testament for the early followers of Yeshua either. They only had the Old Testament, filled with prophecies about him."

The prophecy in *Isaiah 53*, written in 700 BC, is the most explicit about his death and the purpose of his death. If you have never read it before, please do so, and read it with this in mind. First, Yeshua took upon himself all of humanity's failures worthy of the worst kind of punishment. He took this while wearing the Crown of Thorns they had put on him to mock him as "King of the Jews", and yet, by his suffering and eventual death, he regained the power and overcame even death so that he could restore our crowns. Many other prophecies could fill up the following pages, but this is not intended as a commentary book but a journey from darkness into the light until the last breath.

The price for Yeshua to wear this Crown of Thorns meant a life of a suffering servant, which was the same price paid by his closest disciples. Ten of the twelve were martyred and killed in cruel ways. The path is narrow, and that's why only a few find it because few will dare to walk through the narrow gate. There is a path for "whosoever" and they can receive blessings. However, the path of those whose deepest desire is to hear the very pulse of God's heartbeat and walk intimately with Him is narrow, and it comes with a price. It means loving those who hate you, blessing those who curse you, praying for those who spitefully use and abuse you, loving those who steal from you, and those who turn their backs on you and abandon you. It means continuing to love and pray for them, forgiving those who persecute and betray you, and even those who may put you to death.

Please pause and reflect the next time you approach the rose and the thorns. Ask yourself: what are the things in your life that are stiff, defensive, and prickly and far away from the love of God? Then, contemplate deeply on Yeshua's final words on the cross, **"Father, forgive them for they know not what they do."**

When we wear the crown of God's love and allow it to enter every area of our lives, the reward is a crown of twelve majestic, priceless stones. These stones cannot be purchased by any person through their own efforts. They are the rewards of walking the path of love, forged from the most glorious light, earned through a life laid down and enduring until the very last breath.

The first jewel on this crown is **Jasper**, which speaks of the level of brightness and the intensity of the power of your light. This radiance comes from your everyday acts of goodness, the little actions that accumulate every day of our lives. It could be a smile, a hug, or a comforting letter that we write.

"Let your light so shine before men,

that they may see your good works and glorify your Father in heaven."

-   Gospel of Matthew 5:16

Sapphire is the second, vibrating according to the intensity of the *truth and honesty* you live by. The light colour is the most beautiful blazing blue, with the very sound and power of truth expressed by every word and gesture.

"But let your 'Yes' be 'Yes,' and your 'No,' 'No.'

For whatever is more than these is from the evil one."

- Gospel of Matthew 5:37

Three things cannot be long hidden:

the sun, the moon, and the truth.

- Buddha

Chalcedony is the third stone, and its colour is turquoise beaming light, one that emits eternal living *patience*, the type of patience that endures until the end, with its light that revealing the suffering that one has had to endure and radiates the deepest level of calm in any situation.

"Let's not get tired of doing good, because in

time we'll have a harvest if we don't give up."

- Galatians 6:9

Emerald is the fourth stone, and its colour is a majestic bright beaming green that speaks of your life-giving actions of *kindness*.

Then the King will say to those on His right hand, 'Come, you blessed of My Father, inherit the kingdom prepared for you from the foundation of the world: for I was hungry and you gave Me food; I was thirsty and you gave Me drink; I was a stranger and you took Me in; I *was* naked and you clothed Me; I was sick and you visited Me; I was in prison and you came to Me.'

- Gospel of Matthew 25:34-36

"But I say to you, love your enemies, bless those who curse you, do good to those who hate you, and pray for those who spitefully use you and persecute you, that you may be sons of your Father in heaven; for He makes His sun rise on the evil and on the good, and sends rain on the just and on the unjust" (Yeshua)

- Gospel of Matthew 5:44-45

Sardonyx is the fifth, which manifests in the most potent bright clear white light and speaks of one's *purity* and ability to stay clear from everything that pollutes us.

To the pure all things are pure, but to those who are defiled and unbelieving nothing is pure; but even their mind and conscience are defiled.

- Titus 1:15

Hard it is to understand: By giving away our food, we get more strength, by bestowing clothing on others, we gain more beauty; by donating abodes of purity and truth, we acquire great treasures.

- Gautama Buddha

Sardius is the sixth stone, appearing as a honey-coloured red, blazing through a marvellous light, and speaking of the *unconditional love* that is born from the sacrifice of not wanting anything in return. It is what we should do towards all of God's living creatures, much like the bee going back and forth, collecting nectar to make just a teaspoon of honey.

Greater love has no one than this, than to lay down one's life for his friends.

- Gospel of John 15:13

Chrysolite is the seventh and is a bright golden yellow and speaks of your *faith* and your ability to trust, especially in the most challenging testing times.

Now faith is the substance of things hoped for,

the evidence of things not seen.

For by it the elders obtained a *good* testimony.

- Hebrews 11:1

Beryl is the eighth and is connected with the ocean and varies from aqua green to blue, but in heaven, it appears as light blue, transferring the most radiant *peace*. A peace that enters a home and fills a house with a transferable living peace.

Blessed *are* the peacemakers,

For they shall be called sons of God.

- Gospel of Matthew 5:9

"There is also a heaven upon earth in our own breasts.

Do not seek it without, but within your heart ;

then you will not come into heaven for the first time when you die,

but remain in it always."

- Wilhelmine von Hillern

Topaz is the ninth stone and resembles the bright, radiant color of the sun, beaming out with rays of the vibration of *joy*. Joy is a powerful force because wherever it goes, whoever it touches can be lifted in spirit. Joy is the overflow of our gratitude. When we are deeply grateful, we cannot hide our joy.

Continue earnestly in prayer, being vigilant in it with thanksgiving.

- Colossians 4:2

Chrysoprasus is the tenth stone and resembles the green of grass fields and forests, speaking of how we use our skill sets, knowledge, and understanding of the *wisdom* we have been given. Did we use them to benefit all sentient beings, or did we use them to gain wealth and glorify ourselves? King Solomon was often seen wearing these colours, and if you ever have the chance to meet him, you will see a green radiance pouring out of him.

Wisdom *is* the principal thing;

Therefore get wisdom.

And in all your getting, get understanding.

- Proverbs 4:7

The middle path is the way to wisdom.

- Rumi

Jacinth is the eleventh stone and appears as a beautiful, majestic light, radiating in a brown colour as though the Earth's natural colour was illuminated through light. It speaks of *humility* and the ability to surrender or to be corrected, the opposite of pride. Thich Nhat Hanh is a soul who indeed wore this precious stone close to his heart.

With all lowliness and gentleness, with longsuffering,

bearing with one another in love.

- Ephesians 4:2

True love is a process of humility, of letting go of our individual ideas and notions to embrace and become one with another person or our entire community.

- Thich Nhat Hahn

Let this mind be in you which was also in Christ Jesus, who, being in the form of God, did not consider it [b]robbery to be equal with God, but made Himself of no reputation, taking the form of a bondservant, *and* coming in the likeness of men. And being found in appearance as a man, He humbled Himself and became obedient to *the point of* death, even the death of the cross.

- Philippians 2:5-8

Amethyst is the twelfth stone and is the colour of the robe they placed around Yeshua when they mocked him - it is purple and speaks of one's *servitude*. It was the colour they put around kings and royals. The true King came as a suffering servant, but they couldn't recognize him except those with eyes to see and ears to hear. The colour is reflected as the most majestic light purple and speaks of our ability to serve. Even though Yeshua came in authority and power, he never abused that power, always choosing to help the poor, the broken, the needy, the blind, and the suffering.

"Whoever wants to be a leader among you must be your servant, and whoever wants to be first among you must be the slave of everyone else. For even the Son of Man came not to be served but to serve others and to give his life as a ransom for many."

- Gospel of Mark 10:43-45

The greatest among you must be a servant.

- Gospel of Matthew 23:11

So let's make our lives count, and whatever we sow here, we will reap in the next as it is a true reflection of our life and time spent here. These are our true heavenly virtues brought about by our actions on earth. They are our real treasures, the marks and rewards of our efforts and the only treasures we can take with us when we pass on, not the ones that will rust away or can be stolen from us.

Store your treasures in heaven, where moths and rust cannot destroy,

and thieves do not break in and steal. Wherever your treasure is,

there the desires of your heart will also be.

-   Gospel of Matthew 6:20-21

My Prayer for You:

May your crowns bear the stones of goodness and reflect the truth of the Logos and the Rhema, the living Word of Truth that is sharper than any double-edged sword. May it be carried by the patience that endures from the many trials and tribulations you may encounter, waiting patiently for "Thy will" to be done and not from selfish desires. Walk always with kindness that sees how true light sees, with no judgments or condemnation but a loving hand always ready to help. And with the purity of your hearts, may you see past the many veils, walls, and masks that souls erect during their time away from God's eternal love. May you experience the joy of laying our lives down as service always, with faith and trust to hear, so you can better help others to safety and peace, always in gratitude and joy, applying and sharing the food of God's wisdom with all sentient beings. May you remain with a humble heart that is easily corrected when mistaken and become a joyful servant willing to stoop low to wash the feet from the mud of this world that stains our lives, but with the courage and boldness of a lion roaring with God's unconditional love.

Amen

YOUR NEW NAME

It has been given to you to know the mysteries of the kingdom of heaven.

- Gospel of Matthew 13:11

As one begins to form a more intimate union with the presence of The All, some mysteries are whispered and revealed. In ancient texts, names hold a significant role in the heart of God and our lives. So therefore, when I named my three children, I prayerfully inquired about what names would best suit their characters

Sara is our eldest, the first to arrive, but she came with an unusual arrival. One very early morning, I was awoken and heard the inner voice speak to my spirit, *'Prepare, because you shall have a girl, and her name shall be called Sara.'* I immediately told my wife, and Sara was born within a year of that word. It was strange that my in-laws wanted us to give her a different name, but I told them the name was given and would suit her character. I did the same with our middle son (Nathaniel) and youngest (Daniel). What's impressive to see is that they all carry and live out the essence and fragrance of their names.

Often you find that names are changed, or people receive new names, e.g. Abram's name was changed to Abraham (*Genesis 17:5*), as was the name of his wife, Sarai, changed to Sarah (*Genesis 17:15*). Both names went from Sarai meaning "my princess," to Sarah, indicating a "universal princess". She was not only blessed with a child at the age of ninety but also to all the nations that would come through her (*Genesis 17:16*); As did Abram, who became a father of many nations after being given a new name from God when he was one hundred years old already. From his seed, the tribes of Israel and Ishmael came. So, Abraham's name change was very significant to his calling and purpose. And this applies to us now too. When we let go of *me, myself* and *I* life, we enter a union with our Maker, and our names shift from "I" to "Our". And this is the first change that needs to occur in our lives.

Then Jesus said to His disciples, "If anyone desires to come after Me, let him deny himself, and take up his cross, and follow Me. For whoever desires to save his life will lose it, but whoever loses his life for My sake will find it.

- Gospel of Matthew 16:24-25

We can see this in the life of Jacob, who spent the whole night wrestling with God (*Genesis 32:22-32*). God was trying to teach him the lesson of letting go and to see a bigger, more effective plan that He had for Jacob's life, rather than the narrow vision that Jacob clung to. Unfortunately, Jacob couldn't perceive the all-encompassing plan that the Almighty had prepared for him before the foundations of the earth. This often happens to all of us for various reasons - we lose trust in ourselves, others, and sometimes in life itself, causing us to formulate plans through a protective or fearful lens. These plans can often harm ourselves and others as we try to fulfil them, leading us to either die in our pride or, like Jacob, fight or wrestle until we eventually tire of the suffering and strain.

Once Jacob realised it was a blessing, his grip and alignment changed. And thus, his name was changed from Jacob (meaning *supplanter*) to Israel (meaning *one who prevails with God* or *triumphant with God*). And so will your name and life change once you realise the way has been prepared for you, and all you need to do is surrender and yield.

Through struggle and suffering, we too eventually tire of our egos and the suffering they cause. Like Jacob, we wrestle until we give up the fight. But only when we surrender will we perceive the bigger plan that our own egos prevent us from seeing. In the dimensions of Heaven, or the Kingdom of God as Yeshua calls it, this is the first name change we all must experience. Our flesh is weak and always wants to walk in its own way, while our spirit is willing. That's why we are taught this beautiful prayer when wrestling with our ego selves: *'Not my will, but **Thy** will be done.'* We must surrender to a co-working, merging partnership with every living creature and not to our self-seeking egos.

Let us all embrace this loving path for our lives, so we can better discern His ways and purposes, established before the very foundations of the earth. Your name has been whispered and breathed, and in that breath, your name's purpose was intended. You are carrying that purpose and waiting to fulfil your destiny.

The truth is, the longer we wait, the more ingrained our patterns and habits become, making it harder to change. The ways of God for your life are not just for your benefit, but rather, we should live out the prayer of sincere Buddhists who pray, *'Let me live here for the benefit of all sentient beings.'* How beautiful is that? Let our lives be a blessing to every creature, great and small. This is a truly authentic way to live. How fortunate we are to have souls like Yeshua, Buddha, Moses, and Mary grace the earth with their sweat, blood, and tears.

A message to Christians regarding the title 'Whosoever,' a word, name, and title that Yeshua often used to invite anyone and everyone to the blessings of the Heavenly Kingdom. The word 'Whosoever' is significant because it implies that the blessings are given to those who demonstrate actions acceptable to God, rather than simply carrying the label of Christian, Jew, Muslim, Buddhist or Hindu. Therefore, let us delve deeper into the text to better understand this word/title/name 'Whosoever.':

Whoever seeks to save his life will lose it, and whosoever loses his life will preserve it.

- Gospel of Luke 17:33

Assuredly, I say to you, whosoever does not receive the kingdom of God as a little child will by no means enter it.

- Gospel of Luke 18:17

I have come *as* a light into the world, that whosoever believes in Me should not abide in darkness.

- Gospel of John 12:46

Therefore, whosoever hears these sayings of Mine, and does them, I will liken him to a wise man who built his house on the rock: and the rain descended, the floods came, and the winds blew and beat on that house; and it did not fall, for it was founded on the rock. "But everyone who hears these sayings of Mine, and does not do them, will be like a foolish man who built his house on the sand: and the rain descended, the floods came, and the winds blew and beat on that house; and it fell.

And great was its fall."

- Gospel of Matthew 7:24-27

"Not everyone who says to me, 'Lord, Lord,' will enter the kingdom of heaven, but only the one who does the will of my Father who is in heaven. Many will say to me on that day, 'Lord, Lord, did we not prophesy in your name and in your name drive out demons, and in your name, perform many miracles?' Then I will tell them plainly,

'I never knew you. Away from me, you evildoers!'"

- Gospel of Matthew 7:21-23

So, let's go back to the topic of names and their importance in a text. Here are some other reasons why your name is important and how it will also affect the new spiritual name given to you. Sometimes the text can reveal a name with prophetic insight into a person's life. For example, Yeshua means **God saves** and Buddha means **Awakened one**. The name Abraham means *Father of many nations*. Sometimes these names are mentioned as names or titles, as in *Isaiah 7:14*, where it says, *"Therefore the Lord will give you a sign: The virgin will conceive and give birth to a son, and call him Immanuel."* The name Immanuel means "God with us." In *Isaiah 53*, he is called the "suffering servant," like the description of God who walks with us as a Helper, leading us into all Truth.

But the Helper, the Holy Spirit, whom the Father will send in My name, He will teach you all things, and bring to your remembrance all things that I said to you.

- Gospel of John 14:26

Names often convey a spiritual message as a reminder of past, present, and future events. For example, the name 'Moses' means *'to draw out'* or *'to deliver,'* and by saying his name, we are reminded of how he delivered the Hebrews from Egypt in a prophetic and powerful way. Sometimes, a new name is given to establish a new path. For instance, in *Acts 13:9*, Saul is called 'Paul' for the first time on the island of Cyprus. Often, names reveal something about the character or temperament of the person or place. They can also provide crucial information about genealogies, historical succession, continuity, legitimacy records, and unique information about families, past and future promises, and legal rights.

To conclude, Simon, who became one of the twelve original students of Yeshua, had his name changed to **Peter**, a nickname. It means **rock** (*Petros* is the Greek word for "a piece of rock, a stone"). The nickname was significant for him and his fellow brothers because he had been the type of character who would often say one thing and do the opposite. You might remember him saying, *"I will never be the one to betray you, Yeshua."* Then he did it three times. He often gave advice, running away with his emotions rather than thinking about things. So, giving him the name of a rock reminded him of being rooted, earthy, solid, down to earth and not over-reactive and over-emotional. Yeshua would often do this by name or by circumstances to allow you to look into the mirror of light so that you could be aware of your weakness and run away to be led by pride. He gave Judas the responsibility of looking after the finances, and I believe he wanted him to overcome his lust for money, which he couldn't, even to his last breath.

YOUR SPIRITUAL NAME

He who has an ear, let him hear what the Spirit says to the churches. To him who overcomes I will give some of the hidden manna to eat. And I will give him a white stone, and on the stone a new name written which no one knows except him who receives it.

- Revelation 2:17

A beautiful, bright, and magical new name is promised to those who overcome, written on a white stone with some hidden manna. This personal, sacred name will be revealed to you alone in the secret place and intimacy with the great I AM.

This name is reserved for you and God in the sacred, pure holiness of His and your private space. It is the most beautiful thing we all secretly desire, buried beneath all the layers we, unfortunately, get attached to and quickly forget about. But I can reveal how and why the name will be whispered to you and how it leads to a new gateway into a new life and dimension. Before I wrote these pages, I was very cautious, repeatedly checking to ensure it was something I could and should share.

Firstly, there are three critical parts that must be understood before receiving this blessing. The first is understanding what it means to overcome in the way God sees it. The second is understanding and accepting the hidden manna. And the third is the white stone. These are the three elements that must be known before being given a name with the sacred stones. It's essential to note that this name can only be given by God. No one else has the authority, purity, or place to do so. If anyone writes or tells you that they have this authority or permission, it's a fabricated lie from their egoic desires. This name can only ever be transferred to you by the One who sees into the depths and intentions of your heart, the One who knows every secret thought you have.

The first key in this threefold cord is to overcome, which can mean to conquer, subdue, or get the better off and is typically used to describe a victory in some form of battle. Yeshua again uses these words with another promise:

"To him who overcomes I will grant to sit with Me on My throne,

as I also overcame and sat down with My Father on His throne."

- Revelation 3:21

A promise to sit with him and enjoy his union if we overcome. So, what is overcoming that we are all called to do? Remember, the text often uses the number three: the Way, Truth and Life; knowledge, understanding and wisdom; Peter, James and John.

In this text, the words "overcome", "manna", and "white stone" are used in the context of "three" because we are made up of *body*, *mind*, and *heart*. A complete experience cannot be limited to just the mind or the heart, but must be lived and experienced in all three aspects. We may hear and receive the truth, but it is only when we walk in the truth that it becomes a real manifested life experience. Therefore, to overcome something completely, it needs to be a threefold experience. The following text confirms this threefold battle that we must all overcome, just as Yeshua did:

Do not love the world or the things in the world. If anyone loves the world,

the love of the Father is not in him. For all that *is* in the world—the lust of

the flesh, the lust of the eyes, and the pride of life - is not of the Father but is

of the world. And the world is passing away, and the lust of it; but he who

does the will of God abides forever.

- 1 John 2:15-17

We are called to love God and all sentient beings and align our bodies, minds and hearts to Him as the first two commandments instructs us. So, the world and the attachments of this world are what we are all called to overcome. Not because we are not meant to enjoy our lives here but instead being dragged and controlled by three things. The **lust of the flesh**, the **lust of the eyes** and the **pride of life**.

We are first called to love God and then all sentient beings, not replace them with things that fuel and intensify our cravings, forming destructive habits that we quickly become attached to and even kill for. When John speaks about the "**lust of the flesh**," the word translated as "lust" means "inordinate desire." Any desire that goes against God's will and heart is considered lust - the part of us that seeks to be selfish, putting our needs and desires above everything and everyone, even if it causes pain and suffering to ourselves and those we love dearly. The lust of the flesh is a self-centred life that only sees as far as its own selfish cravings, which are constantly burning if the fire is not quickly put out. That is why lust is often compared to fire because it can quickly spread throughout our entire life. The second phrase, **"lust of the eyes,"** describes a burning desire for what we see and want. Our eyes are the way we perceive things and the gateway to our soul; light is first received through our eyes. In the Gospel of *Matthew, chapter 6, verse 22*, Jesus describes the eye as the lamp of the body:

> *"If your eye is bad, your whole body will be full of darkness."*

Your eyes are closely related to the desires of your heart. If your heart is longing, craving, and lusting for things it sees, your eyes will follow, and shortly after, your actions will too. The lust of the eyes describes a soul that is overwhelmed by what it perceives from the external material world, such as a neighbour's house or suite. An intense craving pulls them into what they see and away from the true light of the indwelling spirit.

The third phrase, "the pride of life," describes one's attitude of self-importance. It speaks of the desire to be deeply recognized, arrogant, constantly bragging about one's status or achievements, and the opposite of humility. Anything we pride ourselves upon is the pride of life. This egoic arrogance, along with our false ideas and constructs of how great we think we are, wrong views we have adopted about ourselves, and clinging to our sense of superiority are the three biggest traps that pull us away and separate us from our eternal true nature, our true image and likeness. Yeshua overcame these traps in the wilderness and every 24-hour cycle that he spent on Earth, and he is now calling us to do likewise.

To overcome, in God's mind, is to conquer the world by overcoming the ***lust of the flesh***, the ***lust of the eyes***, and the ***pride of life***. When we do, we will be granted hidden manna, the pure living bread of life made from the purest light of His wisdom, the eternal living sound-word vibration that creates in us a stone of pure, radiant diamond symbolic of a new heart without any traces or imprints of our struggles of *old age, suffering, or transgressions (sin)*. This transformed heart will be filled with the pure radiant light of His pure carbon Eternal Love. It has to be a new heart because no other spirit can carry the Sacred Name of all names unless it is purified and touched by His light. No soul will be able to sing or have His Name. His very expression is above every power and frequency, above every other name in purity and holiness, love and glory, compassion, and peace. We won't be able to carry this presence with our earthly hearts that have overcome, because it is reserved for the higher dimensions of our next life, but only if we overcome, finish the race, and breathe our very last breath with the sound of victory.

UNTIL THE LAST BREATH

Many of us have lost loved ones, some more than others, and some still experience the grief of losing a loved one. As we come to the final chapter of this book, I would like to share a true story that sums up the closing chapter of all our lives.

I have lost some very close friends during the past four years (ironically, during the COVID-19 period, but not because of it). One, in particular, was a lady who had recently retired and had sought my help with life coaching. I had been helping her for around seven years with intensely personal issues that primarily occurred while she was married. She suffered a painful divorce that caused so much trauma for her and her children. She was courageous and prepared to confront and correct all of her mistakes.

Then, around the seventh year of our walking together, she was diagnosed with Amyotrophic Lateral Sclerosis (ALS), commonly referred to in the U.S. as Lou Gehrig's disease, a disease broadly made known to the public through Stephen Hawking. This crippling neurodegenerative disease results in day-to-day progressive loss of motor control of voluntary muscles. Early symptoms include stiff muscles, twitches, gradual weakening, and muscle wasting. In the last year of her life, she was unable to speak as she had lost control over her tongue. As she moved abroad to be closer to her daughters and grandchildren, we would communicate via text messages and zoom, using hand gestures and facial expressions, and relying on keyboard typing.

This courageous woman stared death in the face for her remaining days while the body that served her all her life was slowly wasting away. She was losing all of the freedom we take for granted, like breathing, speech, and unrestrained movement because at times, she could not even lift her head and would gasp for air.

I have walked with people from all walks of life and have had many years of experience holding their hands up to their last breath before they depart. It is never easy, but it is a great honour and privilege to be a part of the process. We had spoken about death and the best way to prepare and lead up to it. She had mended, forgiven, and found peace in every area of her life, and was ready to say goodbye in the way that I had taught her, as Guru Ma taught me. Death is something we are prepared to handle when we are in correct alignment. During her final days, I tried my best to fly over to Holland where she was residing, but was refused entry at the airport due to all the travel restrictions. As I couldn't fly over, we agreed to do the live Wednesday regular guided meditation class for her, and about fifty people joined me. I started the guidance in a sacred and slow rhythm, knowing she could hear my every word as her family placed the laptop beside her. Finally, after the meditation, she fell into a deep and peaceful sleep. She woke up the following morning with her daughters by her side, motioning and messaging to speak with her brother. She had sent me a message saying, "Steve, I know what to do." Her daughters later told me that she lay back and left peacefully soon after she had spoken to her brother.

You may be asking why I am sharing this with you. It is because I want you to know that life and death are intimately joined and woven together. How we live our lives every day, in every 24-hour cycle, will determine the condition in which we depart. I have walked this process and studied death for many years, closely observing and connecting how every strand in our lives has an influence, a course, and an effect until our last breath.

We arrive on Earth, floating from the waves and particles of the light of God's mind, and into the dark, unknown yet safe and vulnerable womb of our mothers. Our bodies, every part, cell, and hair, form precisely without effort. The shape and colour of our unique eyes, hearts, minds, brains, ears, and mouths, every minor detail forming without effort, are connected via a cord to our mothers. Life happens daily, every week, as we are being carried, formed, fed, and looked after by the invisible process we describe as life. This life has a light and works with a plan for all to see, shaping, forming, constructing, knitting together, and placing every part in its designated position. Without light, there can be no life. Light is the primary energy source that maintains and sustains our lives. Imagine removing the light of the sun. So, this light, forming, measuring, and placing have a way and a truth. What do I mean by a truth? Your neck has a truth in how it is upheld, as do your sleep and posture. You will suffer muscle pain if you move your neck incorrectly and remove it from its correct integral position. Light, the source of life that formed you in your mother's womb without effort, has a way for you to walk and express your life. That's why you think, sing, and feel as you do, with your own authentic, raw, and pure expression that only you can express.

Light has a way and a truth which you call your *life*. But upon closer examination, we soon discover that this light (life) was granted to us as a gift, that it was never truly ours, but rather a life borrowed for a while before it returns, before we say goodbye and take our last breath. And everything we fight for, accumulate, hold onto, or grab, no matter how strong or powerful we are, we will still have to let go. We have all discovered at some point that holding onto anything in our lives, except for some good memories, doesn't benefit us. The truth is, it only causes further suffering because everything is constantly changing, just as your body changes at every moment.

Siddhartha Gautama started his life in 564 BC, more than 500 years before Yeshua. He was born a prince to Queen Maya and King Suddhodana, the leader of the Sakya clan in the kingdom of Kapilavastu in Kosala, which is in modern-day northern India. The palace walls protected Siddhartha but also blinded him from the outside world. One day, he ventured out of the palace walls and encountered an elderly, sick person, and a corpse. This realization of the reality of suffering on planet earth caused a deep yearning to find answers to the cause and the way out of these sufferings. He left his family, wife, child, and all his royal responsibilities to search for and find the best teachers and yogis who could teach him their methods to find the path that would lead out of suffering. He underwent some of the most rigorous training for six years, taking his body through intense training and prolonged fasting, taking asceticism to an extreme, and often coming close to death by starvation. Then, one day, seeing his emaciated body, a woman gave him a bowl of milk-rice pudding, ending his six years of asceticism. This act of kindness caused Siddhartha to find the middle way and attain enlightenment after 49 days of sitting under a Bodhi tree. When asked who he was, he would answer and say, "I am Awake" (translated as "Buddha"). After becoming enlightened, he dedicated his whole life to teaching this path to enlightenment. Siddhartha was just like me and you, a normal human being with a deep longing quest for answers about life, death, suffering, and the way out of suffering.

So, let's go into what the Buddha taught and his final words to his close student monks. In them, contain wisdom for our life and preparation for our departure from this earth into the next.

"Work out your own salvation with diligence."

- Translated from Pali Text

Or another translation:

"Conditions are subject to ceaseless change, strive onwards with care."

Let's observe these three beautiful eternal truths:

1 – All component things in the world are changeable.
Everything will surely change, no matter how fixed, solid, or old it may appear. It changes into another form because everything that is living is constantly under this law. That's why he realized that when we do not understand this law, we suffer a lot more. If everything changes, moving from one form to the next, what is the use of trying to hold on? Can you hear the whisper of love in these words to let go, surrender, and allow life to breathe you?

2 – Impermanence.
Everything has its time of death here. No matter how much we choose to cling to the idea that it will last forever - it will surely come to an end! So maybe you can connect these

words with the words of Yeshua when he said in the *Gospel of Matthew 16:24-26* - Yeshua gives his disciples a riddle saying, "*If anyone desires to come after me, let him deny himself, and take up his cross, and follow me. Whosoever desires to save his life will lose it, and whoever loses his life for my sake will find it. For what does a man profit if he gains the whole world and loses his soul? Or what will a man give in exchange for his soul?*" Can you hear the whispers of Love pointing to a life that allows one to be breathed through, lived through and carried through instead of gripping? I'm sure you can. These are true treasures in our lives.

3 – Work hard to gain your own salvation.
It doesn't say, "work hard to gain a PhD or work hard to gain riches." He says, "Work hard to gain salvation" - salvation based on the law, determined by how well you keep them. He was pointing us to take this as essential in our lives and work with determination and focus. To save ourselves from the things that cause us to not keep the Dharma (*Universal Laws*). To liberate ourselves from the ego's selfish nature so that we could refrain from all killing, stealing, lusting, and from wrong, destructive speech, from intoxicants that are harmful to our minds and essentially, our lives. He said to work hard because this is not easy to do and, at times, feels nearly impossible. That's why I felt this as a prayer, as though the Buddha was crying out and reaching for salvation, with everything he had in him. These are such wonderful words of advice for us all.

Let's now read and observe the last words and prayer that Yeshua prayed for his students, and we will soon discover how linked they are. Before we do, let's remember the words of the Buddha calling his students to work hard at their salvation, and recognize that the very name of Yeshua means 'God is salvation.'

The life of the Buddha was like one whole prayer, one whole intercession, for all of us. And then the incarnation of the very Word appears, carrying the sound and demonstrating the very life of salvation in every breath, in every act. His final act on the cross as the suffering servant was foretold and shadowed by all the prophets. As we reflect on these last seven words, please understand that this act was prophesied again and again from one generation of prophets or visionaries to the next, and it was the calling and heartbeat of Yeshua that he chose before the very foundation of the earth, just as it was the Buddha's calling to fulfill his own. We all have our crowns, which were ordained and established before we came here. We all, like every star, have a purpose and a name. Let's now delve into the final words of Yeshua as he hung on the cross:

The First Word

> "Father, forgive them, for they know not what they do."
>
> -   Gospel of Luke 23:34

How often have we said and done things that hurt others because of ignorance and a profound lack of awareness of others? How often have we invested in something, only to find that we were investing in companies that slaughter animals in very cruel ways? How many times have we killed people with our words, humiliated them, laughed at them, wrongly judged, lied, cheated, or stolen out of ignorance and lack of awareness, and been controlled by a life pulled and dominated by the ego-self? None of us have walked blamelessly, no matter how many acts of kindness we have done. We have all been guilty of missing the mark because of plain ignorance.

So let us remind ourselves that we too have fallen at times, away from what we know love is. And for all the times that we have or will have, there is an act of love, a love blanket that speaks out forgiveness for all the deeds done in ignorance. Life goes before us and says, "Father, forgive them, for they know not what they do." This is so we can be blameless once again and not try to cover ourselves with man-made religions or good works. We can step out of our ignorance and into God's love for eternity. This is why it was called the Good News (Gospel) – while we were ignorant, love stooped down and said, "I will cover them as love always does." This blanket of love is for all of us, every soul seeking forgiveness for all the acts we have committed in ignorance of all sentient beings

The Second Word

> "I say to you, today you will be with me in paradise."
>
> -   Gospel of Luke 23:43

So many people worldwide are driven into a life of crime because they believe that no other path exists for them. I knew some young men living in Stonebridge who were told that the only way to a better life was through crime. Poverty and lack of opportunities can have this effect on young and impressionable minds growing up in problematic areas with single-parent mothers. To all of you beautiful souls who have believed this lie, I want you to see this poor man who turned to a life of crime and, in his last breath, found the one he had been searching for all his life. He was absent from this person, but in his final moments, he turned to them and immediately received the response that only love could say, gasping for its own life. 'Today, yes, here with all your baggage, you are forgiven, and I will take you to where I will be.' Love reaches out continuously in the now, for love is kind, love always sees with eyes that forgive immediately, and compassion seeks only to help and lift souls to their rightful place. So how dare we judge people who have chosen a life of crime without knowing a single fact of their life and suffering? Let us choose to be the hand that helps, not points, and the voice that encourages, not condemns.

The Third Word

"Woman, behold your son. Son, behold your mother."

- Gospel of John 19:26

This is a beautiful reminder to care for our parents, the elderly, orphans, and those in need. It calls us to remember and appreciate the channels of love that have cared for us, nurtured us, and worked hard to raise us, sometimes even when they needed a hand themselves. May we never forget our parents, even if at times, they too went astray. And let us remember Mary, who embodied faith, purity, and was the channel of love for Yeshua to incarnate in. She was falsely accused because few believed or trusted the miracle prophesied by the great *Prophet Isaiah in chapter 7:14*: *"Therefore the Lord himself will give you a sign: The virgin will conceive and give birth to a son, and will call him Immanuel."* The name **Immanuel** means **God with us**. From the womb of Mary, through her life, she became the channel through which the Word became flesh and dwelt amongst us. What an incredible soul, honoured to carry the very treasure and heartbeat of God within her. We are reminded of all the mothers who lay their lives down for their children and the great love and faith they possess to bear life in this world. Let us never lose sight of this and always carry gratitude for them in our hearts, for without them, we would not be here.

The Fourth Word

"My God, My God, why have you forsaken me?"

- Gospel of Mark 15:34

Yeshua is quoting Psalm chapter 22, embracing his suffering and speaking to the Father, who accepted the full consequence of his choice to suffer in this way, taking on the full weight of all the wrong actions that have caused humans to live a life outside of oneness with God. This was the first time Yeshua had ever experienced this condition, a condition we can all feel from living a life outside the love and harmony of God. The absence of God's love in the life of every human being leaves them feeling as though they are forgotten, rejected, cast out, or forsaken. How often have we made others feel this way because we have lifted ourselves in pride, thinking we are more holy, superior, or from a higher rank, caste, or skin colour? How many times have we made not just humans feel this way, but also our trees and all our neighbours here? Can we not see that these words are speaking to all of us? Can you not hear the sound of every child when they are told they are too black, brown, yellow, fat, stupid, or not good enough? And the pain it creates? It tears the heart open with the same cry, "Why have you forsaken me?"

The Fifth Word

"I thirst."

\- Gospel of John 19:28

Being forsaken can leave you wandering, thirsty, and searching back and forth. Yeshua longed for humanity to return to oneness. His final prayer for humanity is recorded in *the Gospel of John, chapter 17. He looked at humanity and said, "Your thirst cannot be quenched by the things of this world. I am the living water; whoever drinks the water I give will never thirst again."* So, let us not drink from the waters of this world, which only give us temporary relief, but instead, let us come together and drink from the living waters that have the power to cleanse and wash our lives, for these waters are undefiled. The waters he spoke of were the currents that run through water, producing a way. So when we pray, "Thy will be done," the same waters will run through our lives, cleaning our feet and path.

The Sixth Word

"It is finished."

\- Gospel of John 19:30

What powerful words, to come to the end of your life and work on Earth. It is done! I have finished my race, and I have endured until the end. I could have easily thrown in the towel, but I have run the good race with my whole heart and completed the task. I am delighted and can now rest because of everything I have strived for. As Buddha said, 'work hard for your salvation.' It was done! Yeshua had given everything. For no greater love than this than to lay down your life for a friend. All the animal and child sacrifices that had taken place trying to reach God, all the false altars, religions that had come and gone with all their deceptions. Yeshua was saying, 'I declare that it is finished. No more, it's done, and anything else is required - no more killing, slaughtering, wickedness, or transgressions.' And yet we still turn away from this completed work, choosing to look away and walk in our own lives.

The Seventh Word

> "Father, into thy hands I commit my spirit."
>
> -   Gospel of Luke 23:46

Yeshua bowed his head and handed over his spirit back to where all life comes from, allowing the breath to flow as intended, without interfering with the natural harmony. He surrendered his very life force to the hands that had carried him every step of the way, hands that he had seen touch and heal so many lives. In his final moments, he was going to release the last let go, something we will all face in our own lives one day.

"It is finished," he said, fully satisfied, wholly contented, and at peace knowing that he had accomplished what he had promised: "The son of man has come to give his life as a ransom for many." He knew that the traces he left behind would be of a life laid down so that others could be lifted.

FINAL CONTEMPLATION

It Always Breathed You

Please find a warm, comfortable place to sit with your spine nice and straight. Allow your heart to be filled with immense gratitude, as though it were being filled with the warmth of the sun's loving rays or the best and most sacred moments you have with a caring friend or loved one. Become aware of your sacred breath, inhaling and exhaling. Can you feel the ocean and the waves in your in-breath and out-breath?

Notice that it is breathing you effortlessly. Life is living through you and for you. No effort is required as you contemplate this poem. It was written from my heart to yours with immense love, a sense of how sacred your life is, and a real sense that you are indeed seen, even if you may not know it. Your life is beautiful, and you are beautiful. I hope that when you read these words, some part of you will begin to feel how loved you are.

Let us now connect the two lives and the last words of Buddha and Yeshua. Firstly, let's contemplate a life that, under the Law of Impermanence, is constantly moving from one thing to the next. Then, let us remind ourselves how quickly time is passing and how much we, and everything else, are changing. Nothing is fixed and solid like we have been led to believe. All things will eventually come to an end, including our own lives. Our time here is short, like a cloud that changes and passes by. Therefore, we should work hard concerning the things that matter, such as our salvation.

Therefore, let us set aside our desire for things that are harmful to us, chasing and lusting after them. In the end, we cannot take them with us on our journey. Instead, let us spend our lives on the things that truly matter, like showing loving kindness to all sentient beings, as Buddha and Yeshua have taught us.

Let us cast aside and let go of everything in our lives that separates us from God's love. Let us learn from those who have left footprints of love, so that we too may walk in their footsteps, fulfilling our highest calling to love all sentient beings as Buddha and Yeshua did. Until our last breath, we can say, "I have run the race and finished. It is done. There is nothing else that I need to do. I have looked after my loved ones and kept your laws, and when I have slipped and fallen, I have quickly turned around and amended my way.

SACRED PRAYER

Father, I entrust myself to your loving hands. I am grateful for the life that you have given me, and for all the wonderful friends, brothers, sisters, companions, and lovely moments that I have shared with them. I am thankful for the beautiful trees, rivers, luminous stars, and animals that have enriched our experience here on Earth.

I commit my breath to you, and I thank you for guiding my steps, even in my moments of ignorance. May your breath continue to flow through me without any interference, and may your love and light flow through me until my last breath.

Amen.

"A new commandment I give to you, that you love one another;

as I have loved you, that you also love one another."

- Gospel of John 13:34

Printed in Great Britain
by Amazon

38689223R00130